THE
ACTION CENTRED
LEADER

John Adair

First published 1988 by
The Industrial Society
48 Bryanston Square
London W1H 7LN

Reprinted 1993

ISBN 0 85290 460 0

© The Industrial Society

British Library Cataloguing in Publication Data

Adair, John *1934*

The Action-Centred Leader.
1. Management
2. Leadership
I. Title
658.4'092   HD38

Printed and bound in Great Britain by
Biddles Ltd, Guildford and King's Lynn

CONTENTS

INTRODUCTION

'I don't understand all this fuss about leadership. You just tell people what to do and they do it!' Fortunately that attitude is fast disappearing. There is now a widespread recognition that what industry, commerce and the public services need are not bosses but leaders.

Leadership as the core of managing well — management through leadership — is the message of this book. The emphasis falls on the simple actions that a leader must take to achieve the task, build the team and develop the individual — hence the book's title, *The Action-Centred Leader.*

Leadership and motivation, the subject of Chapter 2, are closely related. Action-centred leaders are enthusiasts, capable of encouraging and inspiring others by word and example. They have an understanding of people, especially that we are all basically self-motivating. True leadership always works with the grain of human nature, not against it.

In Chapter 3 the nature and practice of good appraisal is considered. Appraisal meets important individual needs as well as organisational ones. The key to success is to have both a good appraisal system and good appraisers and appraisees. Average managers tend to rely too much on the system which is only half of the equation. The action-centred leader knows how to make the system work to the benefit of all concerned.

Appraisals tend to be ineffective if proper targets have not been agreed beforehand. The art of target setting, not least for this reason, comes high on the action-centred leader's agenda. Chapter 4 outlines the way to set targets, so that the larger purpose and aims of the organisation are broken down into achievable steps. Then the priorities can be targeted for action.

Decision taking in the context of action-centred leadership is very much something in which people participate. The action-centred leader involves people in making decisions, solving problems and generating new ideas. They are then committed to implementing them. Chapters 5 and 6, on delegation and decision taking, explore this vital aspect of leadership in relation both to groups and to individuals.

If we cannot manage our time effectively, goes the argument in Chapter 7, we are unlikely to manage anything else. There are some principles and practical tips here about the best use of time for all manager-leaders. Time and people are our most important resources. Managing other people's time well is as essential as managing our own time.

Selecting and training members of the team (Chapters 8 and 9) are responsibilities which action-centred leaders take seriously. They may take advice and help from specialist personnel and training advisers, but they know where the buck stops for developing the individual. Choosing people for the team and helping them to develop their own potential for high performance are central elements in each line manager's responsibility.

Leadership and change cannot be separated. The management of change, the area addressed in the last chapter, is therefore virtually synonymous with leadership. Ordinary managers may still vainly hold that they can maintain some sort of a steady state, but action-centred leaders do not believe that is an option. They know that no organisation can plod along a plateau for ever — it will either go upwards or slip suddenly or imperceptibly downwards. Leadership is about having the courage and skill to take an organisation onwards and upwards, despite all the difficulties that strew the way ahead, to the high ground of great achievement.

This book will be especially valuable to those who have attended — or will be attending — action-centred leadership courses. It draws directly upon the contents of those courses, and also upon the excellent series of practical booklets — 'Notes for Managers' — issued by The Industrial Society which cover 'the human side of enterprise'. It has been my good fortune to work closely with The Industrial Society developing the concept of *The Action-Centred Leader*. Besides pulling all the threads of theory together, it serves as an excellent practical framework for the art of management today.

/ THE MANAGER AS LEADER

The degree and quality of the leadership provided by managers are key ingredients in the success of industry and commerce: management status and management salaries reflect this. Yet, in practice, the development of these crucial managerial and leadership skills is frequently left to chance — as if they could be acquired in the course of ordinary office and work experience, or at school, or in the home.

But these skills require training. We would never employ a driver who had not been trained to drive, yet too many organisations still refuse to accept the idea that managers should be trained to manage and that leaders should be trained to lead. In such circumstances, it is hardly surprising if the workforce lacks motivation.

Of course, some people are born leaders and need little instruction. But the vast majority of those people in leadership positions can (and, if given the opportunity, do) benefit from practical training in what needs to be done to motivate their staff so that the people under them become involved in their jobs and give of their best.

Leadership training is vital, even if the trainees are 'naturals'. In this initial chapter we shall concentrate on the key areas of leadership: the leader's actions with regard to (a) the tasks to be performed, (b) the team responsible for performing them, and (c) the individuals in that team.

Leadership

Too often people who are good craftsmen, chemists, engineers, accountants or salesmen are appointed to be managers but receive little or no training in the art of management. It is little wonder that they sometimes fail or, perhaps, manage without distinction (to put it mildly). Of course managers must have the technical

1

competence necessary to achieve results, but they must also have a different kind of competence: the understanding and skill necessary to get work done effectively by others. In short, they need to be able to lead.

As some of the older methods of motivation become less effective (*see* Chapter 2), the importance of the leader increases. Bonuses and similar financial incentives are limited in what they can achieve — many people are quite happy to accept less money for working less hard, so long as their basic wage is sufficient for their needs. Good fringe benefits and welfare provisions may attract people to an organisation, but they will not have much effect on actual performance. Finally, in many fields the intrinsic satisfaction provided by the job itself is no longer an incentive, because the skills which once gave the job its interest have been eliminated by the advent of the new technology.

More and more, managers have to stand or fall by their performance as leaders. The responsibility for ensuring that people give of their best rests squarely with them. They are responsible and accountable for the work of their subordinates. A manager's aim must be to make full use of his or her subordinates' strengths, abilities and qualities, to minimise the effects of the subordinates' deficiencies, and, where possible, to try constantly to improve the performance of the workforce.

This is the object of effective leadership, and it makes sense both psychologically and economically.

Most people gain full satisfaction out of life only if their abilities are fully used. For them and for the organisation — as well as for the country — it is essential that human resources are not wasted. The way to make sure this does not happen is to train managers to be true leaders.

A working model for the leader

So, how can we improve our performance as leaders?

Basically, our effectiveness as leaders depends on our ability to influence and be influenced by the members of our team in the implementation of a task. In practice this means

- ensuring that the required tasks are always done,
- building and reinforcing the team and fostering teamwork and team spirit, and
- developing each individual member of the team.

2

The successful leader acts in all three areas, often simultaneously (see the checklists at the end of this chapter). The three areas interact with each other as shown in the diagram. The circles overlap: if, for example, the 'task' circle were to be blacked out, so too would be large segments of the 'team' and 'individual' circles. Putting this into words, we are saying that lack of attention to the task causes demoralisation and frustration in the team and dissatisfaction to the individual. One can put it the other way around: achievement of objectives is essential if team and individual morale are to be high.

Similarly, if you black out the 'team' circle the other two are affected: unless the leader ensures that an effective team, with good team spirit, is built the long-term chances of achieving the required results are jeopardised. Likewise, if you black out the 'individual' circle, you see how the effectiveness of both the team and the task-performance are affected.

The 'team' and 'individual' aspects may be looked upon also as storage batteries: from time to time, especially after a period of high pressure, they become exhausted. If this happens a good leader will see that they are 'recharged' by paying them extra attention.

Achieving the task

The need to accomplish the tasks for which the team, unit, department or organisation exists is the primary and most obvious duty of the manager. However, in our zeal to achieve targets, we all too often fall into the trap of 'doing it ourselves' (especially during times of change, as we shall see in Chapter 10). Often, of course, you can do the task better than the staff would, but that is not your job. Managers are there to be leaders, and if you find they are doing these tasks more than occasionally you should stop and think.

The leader's main contributions to achieving the task lie in the following areas:

- being quite clear what the aim is, putting it over with enthusiasm, and reminding people of it often
- understanding how the task fits in with the overall plans of the organisation, in both the short and the long term
- planning how to accomplish the task
- determining and providing the required resources, including

3

human resources, time and authority
- doing everything possible to ensure the organisational structure allows the task to be done efficiently
- pacing progress towards achievement of the task
- evaluating results and comparing them with the original plans and with the overall objectives of the organisation.

Developing individuals

We must never forget that the members of our team are human beings. They have their own needs — to live and express themselves as individuals, to earn enough to provide for themselves and their families, to find satisfaction both at work and at play, and to win acceptance by their fellows. Fortunately for the manager, most of these individual needs mean that team members actually want to get involved in their tasks — they want to be motivated. As a result, not too much work has to be done to motivate people — what is more difficult is to work out how to get it right. We shall come back to the problem of motivating people in Chapter 2, but for now we can note that, if individuals are to be adequately motivated, they:

- must be able to get satisfaction from personal achievement in the job they are doing
- must feel that they are making a worthwhile contribution to the objectives of the team and the organisation
- must feel that the job itself is challenging, is demanding the best of them and is giving them a degree of responsibility that matches their abilities
- must receive adequate recognition for their achievements
- must have genuine control over those aspects of the job that have been delegated to them (that is, once you have delegated something, don't interfere unless you really have to)
- must feel that they, as human beings, are developing and advancing in experience and ability.

Making sure that these needs are met for every individual in the team is possibly the most difficult, and certainly the most rewarding, of our tasks.

4

Building the team

Although organisations employ us as individuals, most of our work is done in teams.

A team is an entity in itself. Just as with people, no two teams are alike. To be a successful leader, you have to understand that your team, as a whole, has its own needs. At all times you must be responding to the team — even if this means that sometimes you are 'leading from behind'. You have to be prepared to represent the team and speak with its voice (although you must be wary of overidentifying with the team).

The key actions of the leader in building the team are:

- setting and maintaining the team's objectives and standards
- involving the team as a whole in the achievement of objectives
- maintaining the unity of the team, and making sure dissident activity is minimised
- communicating efficiently with the team by briefing them face-to-face at least once a month on matters which affect them at work
- consulting the team-members (unless time really does make it impossible) before taking any decision which affects them (*see* Chapter 6).

Walking the job

A vital activity for leaders is regularly to go around the workplace of those in the enterprise, department or section. Not only does it help lessen the 'us and them' attitude, it is a good way of keeping in touch with what is happening and it answers such questions as 'Are decisions being carried out?' and 'Do people understand why things are happening?'

Many managers have become 'too busy' to walk the job, and various forms of technological equipment have made them think they are in touch with their subordinates when in fact they are not. For example, some years ago a lathe operator in Leeds was talking about the old days. He said that, in the past, although the boss of the firm might have been thought to have been an arrogant so-and-so, it was 'much more human in those days'. When asked why, he said: 'He was in front of my machine at twenty to nine every day. Now we never see them — they're so busy talking to each other, attending meetings, looking at paper plans.'

Regularity of visits is important. In these busy days we should mark time off in our diaries for walking the job. Senior people, with many responsibilities, may have to ask their secretaries to ensure that all departments are periodically covered. The need for such a systematism is even more important if you find the personal approach difficult.

The object of the visits is to observe, to listen, and periodically to praise. It is certainly not to correct people, except through the line of leadership — that is, going to the foreman or team leader and asking why something is happening. When talking to an individual it is usually best to talk about the job — it is the job, after all, that is the great link between manager and subordinate.And it is important to discipline ourselves to give adequate praise: it is far too easy to see and comment on what is wrong rather than what is right.

Visits should be entirely informal and unannounced. Good manners demand that one should invite the immediate boss to come around the workplace with you. However, the formation of great trains of intermediate officials should definitely not be encouraged.

Walking the job is more than a great help in motivating the employees: it is also a prime means of checking what the situation really is. Examples are: going with sales representatives to visit customers, discussing experiments in research departments, looking at operating figures displayed on wallcharts in offices, reading letters which are being typed — there is a fine art in knowing where to look. A great retailing managing director once went to visit a food factory to see if it was suitable for supplying his chain stores. After he had been received, he startled everybody by walking around the perimeter fence instead of around the factory. As he left he said he would come back again when the factory had good housekeeping and hadn't had to be cleaned up specially for his visit. By walking around the outside of the factory he had seen all the things that had obviously been cleaned out in preparation for his visit!

'By doing one becomes'

Leaders often fret about whether they have the right personality or set of personal qualities to lead well. This need not be a worry.

We are all born with certain individual talents, and there are others we can acquire as we go through life (although there are some we cannot — like a sense of humour). However, many successful leaders manage perfectly well without any noticeable charisma. All they do is regularly act upon the various questions asked in the checklists at the end of this chapter. If we work hard at these — without trying to suppress our own character or inclinations, or worrying about whether our personality is appropriate — the rest will follow.

To summarise, the job of the leader is:

(a) to achieve the task;
(b) to build an effective and cohesive team; and
(c) to 'grow' and develop each individual, so that each has the satisfaction of knowing that he or she is a valued member of an effective team.

Anyone who can do these three things is an effective leader.

It is encouraging that, as has been proven over the years, by carrying out leadership actions in their own way, becoming more skilful and confident as experience grows, people undoubtedly do become more effective leaders and start to acquire and develop the necessary talents and qualities.

What we do is much more important than the type of person we are. It has been shown time and time again that by doing the right things one becomes a more effective leader.

In other words, 'by doing one becomes'.

Checklist

Achieving the task:

- Am I clear about my own responsibilities and my own authority?
- Am I clear about the objectives of my team now and for the next few months, and have I discussed them with my boss?
- Have I worked out a programme for reaching those objectives?
- Can jobs be designed to encourage the commitment of (a) individuals and (b) the team?

- Are the physical working conditions, layout, equipment, lighting, etc., right for the job?
- Does everyone know exactly what their job is? Has every member of the team, after direct consultation between them and me, been given clearly defined targets and performance standards? Has my boss given the same to me?
- Does everybody know exactly to whom they are accountable?
- Are all leaders accountable for teams of no fewer than four and no greater than 15? If not, can anything be done to rectify this?
- Are there any gaps in those abilities of the team members (including me) that are necessary for the task to be satisfactorily completed? If so, am I taking steps to fill the gaps, by training, by getting additional staff, or by bringing in specialists?
- Am I aware of how my team and I are spending our time? Is it the best way? Do we have the right priorities?
- When I am directly involved with the 'technical' work, do I make arrangements so that the team functions well and the requirements of its members are not ignored or overlooked?
- Do I receive regular records which enable me to check progress and to pinpoint weaknesses and deviations?
- Do I make proper arrangements to ensure continuity of leadership during my absence?
- Do I periodically take stock? Have I achieved the tasks as set? And, if not, why not?
- Do my own standards of work and behaviour set the best possible example to the team?

Developing individuals:

- Have I given to each of my subordinates his or her main responsibilities (expressed in terms of desired results) and standards of performance by which both of us can recognise success?
- Am I giving my subordinates continuing lists of short-term targets for the improvement of their individual performances, each with its own maturity date?
- Do they have the resources (including sufficient authority) necessary to achieve the standards and targets?
- Have I made adequate provision for the training (and, where necessary, retraining) of every member of my team?
- In the event of success, do I make sure to acknowledge it and

build on it? In the case of failure, do I criticise constructively and give guidance on improving future performance?

- Does each individual see some pattern of career (and salary) development?
- Can I remove some controls while still retaining my accountability? For example, can I cut down the amount of checking I do, leaving subordinates responsible more and more for the quality and accuracy of their work?
- Can I delegate more decisions to individuals in the team?
- Do I consult the people affected before I take those decisions which cannot be delegated?
- Can I increase each team-member's accountability for his or her own work? For example, could they write the paper on their own work for the technical journal? And do they sign their own letters?
- Can I give my team-members additional authority? Could all queries on a particular subject come initially not to me but to a member of my team?
- Is the overall performance of each individual regularly (at least annually) reviewed in face-to-face discussion (see Chapter 3)?
- Am I sure that, for each individual, work, capacity and pay are properly balanced?
- If, after opportunities for training and development, someone is still not meeting the requirements of the job, do I try to find a position for them more closely matching their capacity — or see that someone else does?
- Do I know enough about the members of my team to enable me to have an accurate picture of their aptitudes and attitudes at work?
- Do I design jobs and arrange work to make the best use of my individual team-members' aptitudes, skills and interest, so that I involve them and gain their commitment?
- Do I give sufficient personal attention to matters of direct concern to each individual?
- Do I regularly walk the job, visiting each person's place of work to observe, listen and praise?
- Do I know the names and titles of every individual in the team — and use them?
- When I smile and say 'good morning', do I mean it?

Building the team:

- Do I set targets with the team and make sure that everybody understands them (see Chapter 4)?
- Is the team clear as to the working standards (e.g., timekeeping, quality of work, housekeeping, safety) expected of them? Do I 'have a go' at those who fail to come up to the mark? Is the team aware of the consequences of being below standard?
- Is the size of the team (or teams) correct — i.e., between four and 15 — and are the the right people working together? Is there a need for more teams to be set up?
- Do all team leaders get instructions about the 'three circles'
- Do I look for opportunities for building teamwork into jobs?
- Do I take action on matters likely to disrupt the team (e.g., unjustified differentials in pay, uneven workloads, discrepancies in the distribution of overtime)?
- Do I take action to care for the well-being of the team and its individuals, and to improve their working conditions?
- Is there a formal and fair grievance procedure that is understood by all? Do I, personally, deal with grievances and complaints promptly?
- Do I welcome and encourage new ideas and suggestions from the team?
- Do I provide regular opportunities for genuine consultation with the team before taking decisions which affect its members?
- Do I explain decisions, thereby helping people to apply them?
- Do I regularly (e.g., monthly) brief the team on progress, people, policy and points for action?
- Do I accept the valuable part trade unions can play in the formal system of representation? Where unions are recognised, do I encourage individuals in the team to be active members, attend meetings, stand for office, and above all speak up for what they believe to be right?
- Do I accord the official representative of the team the facilities (e.g., training) needed to be an effective representative?

2 MOTIVATION

What is motivation?

Motivation is what makes people do things; but a more important meaning of the word is that motivation is what makes people put real effort and energy into what they do. A simple definition of the term 'motivation' might be: 'Getting people to do willingly and well those things which have to be done.' Any action-centred leader must concentrate on what will motivate the members of the team, and so in this chapter we shall look at what needs to be done by leaders if people are to be motivated and are to achieve their full potential.

The importance of motivation

It has been stated that positive motivation occurs when people give in response to a request, but that motivation dies when people are compelled to surrender to a demand.

Motivation comes about through a combination of many factors, such as leadership and the individual's working environment. The effectiveness of employees — assuming they are given opportunity for good performance and have the necessary abilities — depends upon motivation. However high the degree of technology in our organisation, in the last resort the most important resource we have is people, and so the motivation of those people is crucial. Besides, positively motivated people are happier people, and that should be one of our concerns, too.

Make no mistake about it, it is our responsibility to motivate our teams. We are the people who are best placed to create the correct environment in which team-members will 'grow' and give their best to their work. Of course, certain factors are often beyond our control — for example, pay, terms and conditions of employment, status — but practical experience has shown that team-leaders can provide team-members with the most important motivating factors: recognition, responsibility, and work that is challenging.

Team-members' attitudes and behaviour very often reflect motivation — or the lack of it. Examples of the signs of motivation are: high performance, and the consistent achievement of results; the requisite energy, enthusiasm and determination to succeed; unstinting cooperation in overcoming problems; willingness of individuals to accept responsibility; and willingness, both of individuals and of the team, to accommodate necessary change (a subject dealt with in more detail in Chapter 10). Signs shown by employees who lack motivation include: apathy and indifference to the job; a poor record of timekeeping, high absenteeism, and similar problems; an exaggeration of the difficulties in problems, disputes and grievances; a lack of cooperation in dealing with problems; and unjustified resistance to change.

If your workforce shows the latter set of symptoms, it is almost certainly your fault. Managers frequently deplore employees' lack of motivation and of interest in the company's welfare and their own work. Many employees regard their jobs as nothing more than a way of earning a living so that they can engage their excess energies and talents in their leisure-time pursuits, which are what really interest them. If you blame this on the employees you are getting things the wrong way around: there is nothing wrong with people enjoying their leisure activities, but there is definitely something wrong if their work is such that they regard it as mere drudgery.

Countless jobs that could be repetitive, monotonous and uninteresting are made interesting to the people doing them because their managers recognise and respond to them as individuals. But often jobs that could be both interesting and challenging become drudgery simply because managers fail to recognise the need of human beings to be motivated.

The views of the behavioural scientists

Over the years many behavioural scientists have carried out investigations into what makes people tick. Their results must be approached with caution, but obviously it's worth looking at the knowledge the behavioural scientists have accumulated.

Abraham Maslow's thinking on the subject of motivation is centred on the hierarchy of the individual's needs. The hierarchy is summarised in the diagram (page 15). There are several things to notice. First, the hierarchy is based on needs, not wants. Second, it operates on an ascending scale — as soon as one need is met, the individual 'discovers' the need on the next upward rung of the ladder. Third, we can 'revert back'; that is, people operating at level 4 or 5 may revert to level 2 if a feeling of insecurity takes over. Once this need is met, however, they will return to their former needs level. Fourth, and last, if needs are not met, this is demonstrated in people's behaviour.

Putting it another way, what Maslow is really doing is asking two questions: 'Where do you think you really are?' and 'Where are you going?'

Managers should recognise this ladder of needs, and respond to it. They should create the right environment for motivation of their staff and, to avoid the apathy which inevitably comes when needs are unfulfilled, managers must be able to implement the right action at the right time.

Douglas McGregor picked up Maslow's idea that people's needs can be depicted as a hierarchy (see the diagram on page 15). At the bottom of the triangle are our simplest needs: once they have been satisfied they cease to be strong motivators to action. So, as soon as we are materially secure, our higher needs — for self-expression (including the drive for achievement), for an objective, for self-fulfilment — become paramount. It follows, therefore, that, in suitable circumstances and with proper management, the majority of people can be self-directed so long as they have become committed to an objective they value. They will not only accept responsibility: often they will seek it. Two further points: (a) working is as natural as eating or sleeping; (b) creativity is widely, not narrowly, scattered among the population.

In short, people can be self-motivated. Our task is to create conditions of work in which, and through which, self-motivation can find its release. In situations where this is difficult — for example, when the work is dull and repetitive — higher pay remains the sole motivation, because employees can find satisfaction only outside their work. For economic reasons, therefore, it is sensible to make sure jobs are not boring, or to motivate the people doing them.

13

This is McGregor's 'Theory Y' (see Table on page 17). Too many managers, however, subscribe to 'Theory X'. If we do this — and treat people accordingly — we find out nothing about them and our belief becomes a self-fulfilling prophesy: our subordinates will need close supervision, firm discipline, financial incentive schemes, and so on. If, however, we treat people on the basis of 'Theory Y' we find out what they are really like, and are able to manage them according to their individual strengths and weaknesses.

In McGregor's terms the key is: do not make assumptions, but provide opportunity for achievement, responsibility and creativity, and use talents, abilities and interests insofar as the task allows.

Frederick Herzberg had two questions which he put to many people in different jobs and at different levels. These were: (a) what factors lead you to experience extreme satisfaction with your job?; and (b) what factors lead you to experience extreme dissatisfaction with your job? He collated the answers and displayed them in the form of Table on page 17.

Factors shown toward the left of the table — described by Herzberg as 'hygiene factors' — show a greater potential for dissatisfaction than for satisfaction. Improving conditions in these areas does not create a motivational atmosphere — and, in fact, gives only short-term satisfaction, because the new standards soon become accepted as the norm. In Herzberg's words, 'you just remove unhappiness, you don't make people happy'. We come to much the same sort of conclusion if we look at the first three comments about Maslow's 'needs hierarchy'.

Factors towards the right of the table — the 'motivators', as Herzberg dubbed them — have little to do with money or status: they largely concern achievement and responsibility. These correspond roughly to points 4 and 5 of Maslow's 'needs hierarchy'.

The chart shows that the nature of the work can create both satisfaction and dissatisfaction. The moral for managers is clear: we should pay particular attention to the kind of tasks we are expecting people to do, and, if these are boring and repetitive, we should strive to motivate our people in other ways.

Finally, in our swift tour of the findings of behavioural science, we should look at the rather startling results of the Hawthorne

Experiments, carried out during 1924-27 at the Hawthorne Works of the Western Electric Company, Chicago. The results of changes in the working conditions were as follows:

CHANGES IN CONDITIONS	RESULTS
daywork to piecework	increased output
introduction of five-minute rest periods, morning and afternoon	increased output
rest periods increased to ten minutes	greater increased output
introduction, instead, of six five-minute rest periods	output fell: workers explained that their work rhythm was interrupted
return to two rest periods, the first with a free hot meal	increased output
women permitted to go home at 4.30pm instead of 5.00pm	increased output
all improvements in working conditions rescinded; women returned to 48-hour week, with no rest periods, no piecework, and no free meals	output increased to highest point recorded during entire period

In fact, productivity later settled to a lower level — although it was still higher than it had been before the experiments began. The conclusions that were drawn were that improvements in working conditions will in themselves provide only a short-term stimulus to higher performance, and that in the long run continued improvement is dependent on other factors — such as the extent to which people are allowed to 'grow' within the job.

Although these findings are over 60 years old, many thousands of practising managers have paid them no heed. In their attempts to eliminate variables and predict results, managements have all too often attempted to depersonalise their organisations. 'Scientific management', with its accent on efficiency, believes people are motivated only by material considerations, and, therefore, that their actions can be ordered without regard to individual or collective attitudes and behaviour.

The action-centred leader knows this is not so.

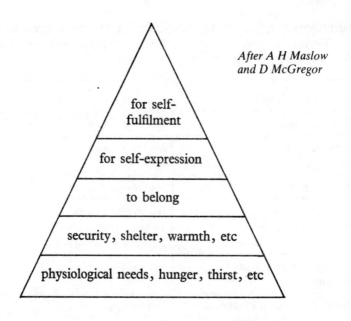

After A H Maslow and D McGregor

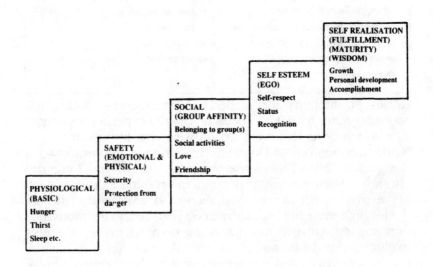

Practical actions which the manager must take

An old saying has it that there are four kinds of people in the world: people who watch things happen, people to whom things happen, people who do not know what is happening, and people who make things happen.

Our job is to make things happen through other people, and so we must be aware of how we can get people to work willingly and well, so that both their own job-satisfaction and the organisation's efficiency are increased. There are four areas in which managers can go about this:

Making subordinates feel valued:

• by regularly monitoring each subordinate's work
• by sharing an interest in your subordinates' lives and in whatever they hold to be important
• by creating an atmosphere of approval and cooperation
• by ensuring that every subordinate understands the importance of his or her individual contribution to the team's/department's /organisation's objectives
• by ensuring that everyone understands the function and philosophy of the organisation and why each team-member's work matters

Providing opportunities for development:

• by setting standards and targets for all subordinates
• by providing on- and off-the-job training
• by arranging any necessary internal and external contacts
• by using subordinates to train others in any specialist skills they may have
• by structuring or grouping tasks to use the subordinates' skills and gifts to the fullest

Recognising achievements:

• by praising individual successes, and communicating the news to others
• by reporting regularly on the team's progress

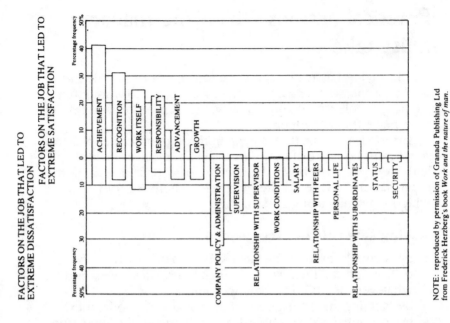

FACTORS ON THE JOB THAT LED TO
EXTREME DISSATISFACTION

FACTORS ON THE JOB THAT LED TO
EXTREME SATISFACTION

NOTE: reproduced by permission of Granada Publishing Ltd from Frederick Herzberg's book *Work and the nature of man.*

Attitudes to work (the X-Y theory)*

Theory X	Theory Y
1 People dislike work and will avoid it if possible	1 Work is necessary to people's psychological growth
2 People must be forced or bribed to put out the right effort	2 People want to be interested in their work and, under the right conditions, they can enjoy it
3 People would rather be directed than accept responsibilities, which they avoid	3 People will direct themselves towards an accepted target
	4 People will seek, and accept responsibility under the right conditions
	5 The discipline people impose on themselves is more effective, and can be more severe, than any imposed on them
4 People are motivated mainly by money	6 Under the right conditions people are motivated by the desire to realise their own potential
5 People are motivated by anxiety about their security	
6 Most people have little creativity—except when getting round management rules!	7 Creativity and ingenuity are widely distributed and grossly underused

*Adapted from D McGregor's The human side of enterprise

18

- by having regular meetings to monitor and give counsel on an individual's progress towards targets
- by explaining the organisation's results and achievements

Providing a challenge:

- by setting and communicating the team's, department's and/or organisation's objectives
- by providing scope for individuals to take greater responsibility
- by encouraging ideas and, where practicable, by allowing subordinates the responsibility to implement them

Motivating change

Change is an inherent part of life, but at work many people — managers and workers alike — actively resist it. Why?

Some of the reasons are fairly obvious, and quite understandable. It is not really change that people are resisting, but the fact that they themselves will have to adjust to the changed situation. Also, they may have perfectly real fears concerning possible loss of job, earnings, skills, status, friends, companions and familiar surroundings. They may be worried in case they will find that they are incapable of adapting to change.

Alternatively, they may be perfectly happy with the prospect of change in theory, but simply believe that the specific changes proposed are deleterious. As the inventor Barnes Wallis once said, 'we are all suspicious of other people's ideas'. A wise manager will listen to the views in this respect of his or her subordinates.

It is all too easy to think of some changes as major and others as minor. Major changes are usually thought of as things like the introduction of new technology, altering pay or bonus systems, making major procedural changes and the introduction of work measurement. Many of us seem to think that other items — such as moving a subordinate from one job to another, making a minor adjustment to the methods of working, modifying the times of breaks or altering canteen prices — are by comparison very minor changes. However, even apparently minor changes can have major consequences, for what you think is a minor change may be a very major one to the individual it affects.

We shall return to the theme of managing change in greater detail in Chapter 10. Here, however, let's look at what is undoubtedly one of the most challenging roles a manager can face: motivating change. The key theme throughout is to be cooperative, willing and flexible — which are, after all, what we are asking our staff to be. While our final objective may never alter, our plan of how we are going to get there may be in a state of constant flux.

How should we go about instituting change? First, we should note a few sentences from the Industrial Relations Code of Practice:

> Communication and consultation are particularly important in times of change. The achievement of change is a joint concern of management and employees and should be carried out in a way which pays regard both to the efficiency of the undertaking and the interests of the employees. Major changes in working agreements should not be made by management without prior discussion with employees or their representatives.

To initiate change, the first thing to do is plan it, taking into account who it will affect and how it will affect them. Then you should arrange for the need for change, and its likely impact, to be explained, by managers briefing down the line to all those affected. Back up verbal briefings by adequate written information and/or instructions. It is vital also to consult frequently those affected (or their representatives): it tells them their views are being considered, and so they will be much more willing to cooperate; it tells you of their specific anxieties, so that you can take these problems into account; and it may bring out important factors which you've previously overlooked.

At all times during change you should review — that is, consider and act on the results of consultation. You should be prepared to reconsider your original plan, arrange for demonstrations of any new equipment, give reassurances of no redundancy or loss of earnings (where possible), and take steps to provide training.

Finally, once the change has been made, you should follow up to see that it has proceeded as planned and that the objective has been achieved. Further consultation, readjustment and communication may be necessary.

At all stages and at all levels, motivation is the key. To sum up, it can come about only if you have the full cooperation of everyone concerned, if you have an effective means of communication which is two-way at all stages and levels, and if there is effective feedback concerning progress made and obstacles encountered. Motivation is especially important and difficult if there is a period during which the change is being effected while present procedures are still, of necessity, being maintained. Here, particularly, the full cooperation of all participants — subordinates, managers, employees, customers, suppliers, trade unions and others — is essential.

Full cooperation is one thing: willing consent is even better. If you are interested in positive motivation, you should be aiming for willing consent.

Motivation at different levels

Exactly how you approach motivation can vary depending upon where you are within an organisation: at the top, in the middle, or at the front line. In this section we shall look at these three in turn. The suggestions are based loosely on studies produced a few years ago by Sir Peter White (once responsible for 63,000 civilians in naval dockyards), Reg Blundell (formerly responsible for 3210 employees as General Manager of British Telecom, Aberdeen and North of Scotland Area), and Allison Grant (catering supervisor with John Sutcliffe and Co. Ltd).

At the top

At the top you deal with people and very little else. Your job is to motivate senior managers who know as much about the behavioural sciences as you do, who have reached their positions by being good leaders, and who have developed the same qualities as you have to the point where they are not going to change much, if at all. This is the level at which 'inspirational' leadership, as opposed to 'mechanical' management, has a very definite part to play. Whether you are successful in that, and thus in motivating your senior managers, will depend very largely on how you have prepared yourself for the top position and the attributes you have acquired in the process.

Specifically, successful motivation at this level will depend on your ability to:

● take responsibility and not duck it
● promote confidence by acting and looking the part

- project a cheerful, hopeful, enthusiastic, encouraging and optimistic image
- avoid fussing, worrying and constant interference
- walk the job and be seen (see Chapter 1)
- set the right example in your personal life
- think positively
- be one of the 'new ideas' people in your organisation
- be seen to be an opportunist
- accept and capitalise on change
- learn new tricks as they come along
- show that you care for those under you
- have the moral courage to take the right decision, even if it's the unpopular one
- have the courage to delegate
- take hard decisions: remove passengers and dead wood
- communicate constantly to all points of the compass
- listen
- avoid needless confrontations
- recognise and deal with stress in yourself and others
- pick winners
- enthuse people — develop your natural charisma
- assuming you can do it naturally, make people laugh.

In the middle

When people are asked what are the qualities they most admire in managers for whom they have worked, the list usually looks something like this:

- they really know the job and do it well
- they never panic
- they tell you exactly what they expect
- you know precisely how you stand with them
- they are fair, and have neither favourites nor scapegoats
- you feel you could never let them down
- you really enjoy working for them

If you are a senior manager, stare into this 'mirror' of personal qualities and ask yourself if you see your own reflection. If the answer is 'yes', you may take modest pride in the knowledge that people will work well and willingly for you.

At the front line

Motiving people at the front line — porters, washers-up, hands — can be helped by treating them as people. Even though they may be doing an unglamorous job, it is essential for motivation that they realise just how important their role is in the operation as a whole, and for the supervisor to gain their respect.

Create a good working atmosphere, and get the people working as a team. The hardest thing is weeding out the odd ones who are not pulling their weight.

Of course, motivation is more difficult if people are doing monotonous jobs all day on their own. Such people may not be the brightest or quickest members of staff, but they are doing a worthwhile job and you really must be genuinely polite and respect their intelligence. To give a person pride in their job, you might do something as simple as give them a smart, respectable uniform, so that they feel involved and a part of the operation. Also, of course, praise a person where praise is due — something often forgotten because that person is far from the spotlight.

Showing concern and interest in the problems of front-line employees, while at the same time being firm and putting them under pressures — for example, imposing deadlines and time limits — can be an extremely effective motivator.

3 APPRAISAL

People cannot be expected to give real commitment to their work unless they know what they are meant to be doing — and why — and what progress they are making towards their objectives. To achieve this, there must be a proper means of ensuring that you and your subordinates meet regularly to discuss how well they are doing, which areas of their work need particular attention, and what their prospects for promotion are.

In this chapter we shall look at how such a scheme can be developed and used, and how the appraisal interview itself should be conducted.

Why appraisal?

A frequent reaction of managers to the suggestion that they should implement a formal appraisal system is: 'Why bother?' They feel they already know the people working for them and their levels of performance. This may or may not be true, but the reaction highlights a lack of understanding of the overall advantage of having such a scheme — for not only will the organisation as a whole benefit from an appraisal scheme but, equally important, there are benefits for the individual.

Let's look first at the benefits to the organisation.

To a large extent the performance of an organisation depends on the way in which its managers use and control the organisation's basic resources — people, space and buildings, raw materials, plant and machinery, and money.

Of all these resources, people are the most important, for the effective use of the other resources depends upon the skill and high performance of the individuals within the organisation. In the past, and to some extent still, managements have attempted to achieve this high performance in a variety of ways: by paying higher wages than other employers in the locality, by introducing

24

incentive schemes, by paying attention to welfare and working conditions, or, last and least, by managing in an autocratic manner.

However, none of these options are necessarily effective in the long term — we have noted, for example, the Hawthorne Experiments (page 16). In any case, it is a waste of time attempting to improve performance unless you are sure which areas should be improved. A realistic appraisal scheme is one means of helping an organisation, and the individual managers within it, to identify both the performance levels of the people and the areas that need improving.

Turning to the case of individuals, we saw in Chapter 2 how the work of the behavioural scientists has highlighted individuals' motivational needs. To recap, most people have the following needs:

- the material requirements for survival
- long-term job security
- to experience comradeship within working and social groups
- a sense of achievement, and recognition by others of that achievement
- the development of themselves in skills and abilities.

There is a connection between the first three areas of needs and old-fashioned motivational strategies, but real motivation comes from the fourth and fifth areas. An appraisal scheme, correctly administered, can help satisfy these motivational needs; for example, it will ensure that you and your subordinate get together regularly on a formal basis away from the workplace to discuss the subordinate's performance, thereby providing you with the opportunity to give verbal recognition. Additionally, a good scheme helps ensure that the appropriate action is taken to assist individuals to improve their present abilities and skills and develop new ones.

In order to find a firm basis on which to build — in terms of identifying performance levels as well as motivating and developing people — individuals need to know the answers to certain basic questions.

- Who is my boss?
- What is my job?
- What standards are expected of me?
- How am I performing in relation to those standards?

- Where do I go from here?
- How do I get there?

These questions are important. The first three are concerned with people's jobs: answering them requires a job description to be drawn up defining people's functions and the levels they are required to attain. You have the immediate responsibility for seeing that these questions are answered — and an appraisal scheme will help you do so. The other three questions are answered during or after the appraisal interview.

We can see, therefore, that appraisal is something that helps both organisations and the individuals within them — which, in fact, means much the same thing.

Aims and benefits of an appraisal scheme

The aims of an appraisal scheme should be threefold:

- to establish the current level of performance in the job and to seek ways of improving it
- to identify potential for development and to aid manpower planning
- to link salary realistically to performance

These are three entirely different aims, and should probably be dealt with separately.

Performance appraisal is concerned with the current level of performance in the present job, covering the total job and not just those items of either outstanding or disappointing performance. It also provides the opportunity to lay plans for future action designed to improve performance.

The identification of potential, although a more difficult area to tackle, is nevertheless important. It helps an organisation place the right person in the right job at the right time.

Third, it is important to relate salary to performance. The results of appraisal can be used as a realistic indicator in determining, for example, merit awards. However, experience has shown that salary itself is not a suitable topic for the appraisal interview, as it almost always becomes the dominant item on the agenda and inhibits productive discussion of performance.

The benefits yielded by appraisal schemes, when properly tackled, affect individual employees, management, and the organisation as a whole. Relations between management and subordinate are considerably improved as a result of the two-way communication reinforced by regular appraisal interviews. The manager gains a greater appreciation of the realities of the subordinate's job, the difficulties and the achievements, plus a greater understanding of the subordinate as a person.

One of the main problems for any manager is the successful identification of individual training needs, for the essence of training is to establish programmes which meet individual requirements within the objectives of the organisation. Properly set up and maintained, appraisal enables the manager to identify these needs.

An organisation's internal management potential is further increased by including the interviewer's estimates of a person's potential and an indication of that person's ambitions within the company. Managerial manpower planning requires this information so that it can develop succession plans and training schedules. Obviously, if a person's ambitions and managerial talents can be correlated with the requirements of the organisation, everybody involved stands to gain a great deal.

The cry of 'if only our policy could be altered to include such-and-such my job would be so much easier' is a frequent one. It must be remembered that appraisal helps to show things as they really are, not as they should be in theory or as management would like them to be. Often enough, policies have been changed as a result of the summation of views expressed during an annual appraisal, and previously inflexible organisation structures have been altered to improve communication between levels of management, to cut out overlaps, and to strengthen weak areas.

Types of appraisal scheme

Many of us dislike appraising the work of our subordinates on a face-to-face basis. Frequently this reluctance can be related to the criteria against which we are asked to assess and appraise our subordinates' work. Four of the commonest methods used today are merit rating, written assessment, management by objectives, and target setting.

Merit rating

Usually, with this method, certain criteria are listed and each is given a rating depending on the quality of performance — for example, excellent, very good, good, fair, poor. The criteria used vary enormously from one scheme to another, but typical examples are reliability, drive, and flexibility. The appraisal form itself is often laid out in such a way that the criteria are listed on a column at the left of the page while the remainder of the page is divided into other columns, each headed by the appropriate rating. The appraising manager simply puts a tick in the appropriate boxes.

There are two major disadvantages to this type of scheme. First, the criteria are normally subjective and therefore difficult to measure, and this frequently causes friction between boss and subordinate — for obvious reasons. Second, experience has shown that most managers are inclined to tick the boxes in the middle of the scale, rather than the extremes of good and bad, with the result that most subordinates are appraised as merely 'average'.

Written assessment

The biggest difference between written assessment and merit rating is that the people doing the appraising are required to write down their views — not just put a tick — against the criteria under consideration. This has the great advantage of making you give more thought to what you want to say and how you want to say it. However, the ultimate success of this method again depends on the criteria and the questions asked and answered. Also, of course, the criteria are still largely subjective, and so also may be some of the written views.

In some cases, merit-rating and written-assessment schemes encourage you to write down your assessments without talking to the subordinate. This renders an appraisal interview meaningless, and the benefits of the face-to-face discussion are lost.

Management by objectives

To minimise the difficulties of 'personality', and therefore subjectivity, in performance appraisal more objective techniques must be used. The technique of management by objectives (MBO) was introduced to provide the necessary objectivity since the results achieved in the job — if measurable or demonstrable — are a very concrete means of assessing performance. After all, it is whether or not a person is attaining the results required of their position which indicates the level of their performance in that job, not what you, the manager, might construe as being good or bad in relation to such subjective qualities as drive or flexibility.

In order to further evaluate and balance an individual's performance level, some organisations began to rank and grade the results achieved against agreed standards of performance by taking into account the degree of importance of the tasks concerned, and the difficulties and resources involved in their achievement.

This practice often overcomplicated the system, and led to MBO falling into disrepute in some organisations.

Target setting

Some organisations measure the performance of individuals through a system called target setting, a simpler form of MBO. This works best when boss and subordinate regularly discuss basic priorities for action. Targets are then set for the subordinate, and achievements are likewise reviewed on a regular basis — perhaps every two or three months.

Records are kept of successes and failures, and these are used at the annual appraisal interview. This ensures that performance is reviewed over the whole year, not just the previous two months, and that shortfalls in performance can be identified and rectified at an early stage, not merely placed on record at the end of a full year as a, possibly expensive, failure to meet an objective.

Target setting is the appraisal scheme which gives the best results, and so in this book it is given a chapter to itself (see Chapter 4).

Introducing an appraisal scheme

If the full benefits are to be obtained from an appraisal system, it is vital that line management is involved in setting up and developing the system. This way the line managers are more committed to the success of the scheme. One of the best methods of going about this is to try out a draft scheme with representative departments, and then include their ideas for improving the scheme. Certainly experience has shown that, if managers are encouraged to give their ideas about appraisal and are consulted on the format of any paperwork (and in particular to use it in trial runs in role-playing exercises), they will help promote the scheme among their colleagues.

Another point when introducing an appraisal scheme is that it is important that the organisation's objectives are made very clear to all its employees. The 'acceptance level' should in any event be reinforced from time to time by careful briefing; but the scheme is likely to gain most acceptance when it is seen to benefit not only individual employees but also the organisation as a whole.

It is important that the scheme should be applied uniformly throughout the organisation. A senior coordinator should therefore be designated to watch over the scheme.

The basic steps which need to be taken before the scheme is introduced involve deciding on the structure of the scheme.

- Who will appraise whom?
- How often will this happen?
- At what time of year will it happen?
- What training is required for appraisers?
- What form will be used?
- What use will be made of the results (for example, in terms of salary, training, manpower planning)?
- Who will monitor effectiveness?

In designing an appraisal scheme, it is worth considering the following points:

What categories of employee are to be included in the scheme?

- Managers and supervisors only?
- Graduates and others showing management potential?
- Technologists and technicians?
- Professional and administrative staff?
- Sales and marketing personnel?
- Clerical grades?
- Skilled hourly paid employees?
- Semi-skilled employees?

Who will benefit from the introduction of the scheme?

- Individual employees?
- Supervisory and line management?
- Personnel and training staff?
- The organisation?
- A group of companies as a whole?

Are the objectives of the scheme quite clear? Will it be able to distinguish among the following?

- Performance since the last appraisal?
- Future potential?
- Development to improve the performance record for the same job over the next year?
- Development for future jobs?
- Salary administration needs, so as to relate reward paid now to proven performance or future potential?

How will managers be able to assess their subordinates' performances?

- By standards of performance set by the manager after discussion with the subordinate?
- By critical incidents?
- By targets set by the manager after discussion with the subordinate?

Who needs to be involved in the assessment of potential?

- The present manager?
- The present manager's boss?
- The management-development adviser?
- The chief executive?

What indicators can be used to establish potential?

- Results?
- Overall performance?
- Any other factors?

A final question that organisations must ask themselves is:
How can interest and enthusiasm for the scheme be maintained?

Assessing potential

An important part of any appraisal scheme is assessing the future potential of the people involved. Ideally, this should be done by linking the information obtained to a succession plan.

Every organisation should be looking ahead, not only at what it will be producing in a few years' time but also to what sort of management structure it will then require. If this is done, it becomes possible to assess which people already part of the organisation will be ready and able to fill new positions that will be created or will become vacant in the intervening period. Mind you, although this helps an organisation's employees to 'grow' as individuals, it will still be right on occasion to 'buy in' expertise from outside.

The main danger in discussing potential at an appraisal interview is that an individual's expectations can be raised to unrealistic heights. When these hopes are dashed, the obvious result is frustration, often followed by resignation. Indeed, it has been argued that discussing potential is too dangerous, and should therefore be eliminated from the interview. However, it is better to risk dealing with the problem than to leave things unsaid: dodging the issue leaves subordinates to draw their own conclusions, which may or may not be correct. People of high potential may feel that the organisation does not recognise this, and may move away, while people of average potential may inadvertently be given the impression that great things are coming their way, and become frustrated when nothing happens.

It is not very easy to assess an individual's potential, but the task can be made less difficult if consideration is given to:

- projection of current performance
- unused knowledge and experience
- ability to see beyond the immediate situation — a quality more colloquially known as vision

Projection of current performance

Knowledge of past and current performance can be used in an attempt to predict future performance. The accuracy of such forecasts can never be certain, of course, and to a large extent will be governed by the amount of evidence available concerning any particular individual, but someone who has consistently achieved targets is obviously a better bet than someone who has not.

Another factor is where the previous performance took place. For example, if a person's performance has not only improved but has done so in different disciplines and environments, that person almost certainly has useful potential. This is not to say, of course, that an individual lacking such varied experience does not have an equal potential; it is just that in the former case there is hard evidence that the person is capable of adjusting to new situations.

Unused knowledge and experience

A person's potential should not be considered solely in terms of their ability to move upwards in their current discipline — becoming a better and better clerk, for example. It should be looked at also in terms of increasing the person's responsibility in their present job, and their capacity for 'sideways' or 'diagonal' movement into a different discipline. A person might not show much potential for development in their current job, but considerable potential if moved into the 'right' job.

Currently unused knowledge and experience should be looked at too, because such attributes might well be harnessed to great general advantage. For example, a managing director's secretary who has previously worked in Fleet Street should be asked to help out also in Press and Public Relations.

Vision

Some managers and supervisors are inclined to be parochial in their view of what is happening at work. Others are able to understand what is happening around them and, as a result, can cope with colleague relationships better. This wider vision frequently indicates the potential for advancement.

Preparing for the interview

The appraisal interview is essentially a dialogue. The appraiser and the appraised take a share of speaking and listening in order to gain understanding of each other's point of view. It is vital that both the manager and the subordinate prepare themselves for the occasion in the best possible way.

The interviewee should be given seven or ten days' notice and be reassured of the purpose of the meeting. At the same time, they should be asked to consider their own performance over the past twelve months, noting both successes and failures as well as any contributory factors that might have been present in either case.

They should also consider whether there are any areas in which they would like to receive some form of job development, such as through being given more responsibility (with supervision in the early stages), by attending an internal or external course relevant to their needs, or through following some form of reading programme to widen their knowledge and enable them to perform more satisfactorily–in other words, anything that might help them get more out of and put more into their jobs. They should note their personal ambitions, both short and long term, as well as any suggestions they might have for improvements. Another thing the interviewee might be asked to consider is the way in which management tackles the job, identifying any areas which frustrate aspects of the interviewee's performance of it.

The manager, too, needs to be prepared. You should study the subordinate's job description as well as the standards of performance which you and the subordinate have together established and updated. If targets have been set and regularly reviewed, the results should be carefully studied. Analysis of the job in this way — taken in tandem with the appraisal form — will guide you as to the points to be raised.

The basis of this analysis should be readily understood by the subordinate, as it relates directly to the job and the objectives and does not depend on any vague general impressions you might have about the individual and his or her performance.

The questions you should ask yourself are:

- what overall results have been obtained by the subordinate?
- which results have been better than forecast, and why?
- which results have not been as good as forecast, and why?

Managers who have noted successes and failures throughout the year, or who work in an organisation operating MBO or target setting (see Chapter 4), will find it comparatively easy to answer these questions. Indeed, you should be able to provide the answers to these questions through your own understanding of the total situation. However, you may not be aware of the contributory factors (often outside the subordinate's control) which, though perhaps not in themselves major items, have seriously impaired the subordinate's performance.

It may prove helpful to discuss the three questions with other management colleagues, but this is better done as a normal practice throughout the year.

You may have one or several objectives for the interview of a particular employee. For example, you may need to

- advise employees what you think of them in general terms
- recognise good work
- discuss areas which need improvement
- discuss the need to improve and develop performance in the current job to meet new needs within the organisation
- establish a baseline for development into a more senior job
- outline subordinates' potential for promotion within the organisation
- show how the subordinate fits into the departmental structure
- ensure that subordinates clearly understand that performance must be improved if they are to remain with the company, and give counsel as to how this improvement may be achieved.

You should have these objectives clearly worked out in your own mind, and should think them through in detail before interviewing each employee.

The appraisal interview

The interview itself should not take place just anywhere. As with any other personal interview, sufficient time — perhaps as much as two hours — must be allocated, and complete privacy and freedom from interruptions must be ensured: for these reasons, managers often use offices well away from their own. The seating should be comfortable, and arranged so as to foster a cooperative atmosphere rather than a psychological combat exercise.

In general, you should not conduct more than two appraisal interviews in any one day, since the mental demands involved in changing approach and attitude from one subordinate to another are considerable.

Particularly when appraising a subordinate for the first time, you should start the interview by setting the employee at ease with a few casual remarks, and by restating the purpose of the meeting. This will help to focus the minds of both of you on the matter in hand.

Very often a useful way to proceed is to ask the individual's thoughts as to how relevant their job description is to the job they are actually doing. This gambit makes it easier for you to relate the points you wish to make in this area — taking into account such things as how the subordinate's views tie in with the organisation's requirements, what training and development is required for the subordinate to progress in the desired direction, and so forth.

Another opening gambit is to ask employees what successes they feel they have achieved during the past year, what they are least pleased with, and why. Here subordinates may over- or underrate themselves, but nonetheless they may produce very pertinent facts and ideas you didn't know before.

The quickest way to kill the interview in the early stages is to start a major argument over a controversial point. The employee should be encouraged to talk freely, so that a cooperative atmosphere is established and disagreements can be aired without rancour. A brief note of points raised during the employee's self-assessment will enable you to pay attention to these later on.

This joint approach (under your guidance) should develop a common understanding of the employee's role and performance, and clarify what can be reasonably developed in the future.

At every stage your questions must be framed carefully so as to draw out the subordinate's reactions and ideas. They should not be questions that solicit one particular answer; nor should they require only a 'yes' or a 'no' — questions like this interrupt the flow and inhibit discussion. Of course, interviews do not always flow easily, but some problems can be avoided. For example, a sudden switch of topic can confuse the minds of both parties: let the topics flow from one into the next.

It is vital that the interview ends on a positive note, so that the employee leaves the room aware of your appreciation of past performance and clear about future action.

The appraisal interview is not a once-and-for-all act, and so you must ensure that it is followed through with a continuing dialogue throughout the year.

After the interview

It is a bad idea to complete the appraisal form during the interview, partly because it would take too long and partly because it might destroy rapport. Completing sections of the form before the interview is also unwise, because you are prejudging issues about which you may not know all the relevant facts. The form should therefore be filled in afterwards, based on your brief notes of the salient points discussed. It should then be shown to the subordinate, who may add further points before signing it to indicate that they have seen it with you.

In any organisation where MBO or target setting (see Chapter 4) is practised, it is worth arranging a subsequent interview to discuss and agree future objectives or targets. It is unwise to attempt to cover these areas during the appraisal meeting itself.

Usually appraisal interviews are held only once a year, but it is often worth holding them more frequently — with new employees, every six months is preferable. In such cases it is helpful at the end of the first meeting to arrange the time and date for the next one.

Where training programmes and so on have been set up for the individual, it's a good idea to arrange a future interview so that the results can be discussed and considered. Where MBO or target setting are in operation, such projects might be short-term objectives or targets, and will be discussed at the performance review, the date of which is agreed when the objectives or targets are set.

It is most important that you take the necessary steps to implement action discussed and agreed during the interview. This action might consist of giving the employee additional authority or supplying additional support or training — either relevant to the current job or with a view to developing potential.

4 TARGET SETTING

Many people are still assessed on the basis of impressive confidential forms filled in by their bosses with spaces for comments on their cooperativeness, loyalty, enthusiasm and the like. It is enjoyable to play the part of amateur psychologist, but it is also exceedingly dangerous. As one manager put it, 'I reckon that whether I get a rise or not depends on how often I say "good morning" to my boss.' A similarly depressing comment was overheard at a business lunch: 'The only people who assess me at my true worth are the Inland Revenue.'

As we saw in the previous chapter, it is important to use a system of appraisal which goes beyond abstract personal qualities and instead allows an objective assessment. Of such systems, the best is probably target setting.

Target setting enables people to be assessed on the basis of performance. If they are consulted before the targets are set, they will become more committed to them and to their achievement, and more prepared to be assessed according to them.

Why does it matter and what's it about?

No matter how efficient our plant or equipment or how great our technical or administrative competence, our most important resource — although often the most underused — is the human one; specifically, in order to get things done, we rely principally upon other people. If our subordinates are to give their best to their work, each of them must know what they are responsible for, what is expected of them, and how they are doing. Making sure that all these things are fully understood is one of the main purposes of appraisal meetings, as we saw in Chapter 3.

So, what exactly is target setting? Target setting is a means of appraisal which allows us to assess and measure performance objectively, as opposed to subjectively. We shall define the word 'Target' in much more detail a little later, but for now we can simply say that targets are priorities — special tasks that need to be achieved over and above routine work.

Unless people have a clear understanding of what they are trying to achieve (which may in fact be quite different from what they spend most of their time doing), what standards they are supposed to maintain, and how effectively targets are being achieved, their overall performance will be significantly lower than it could be. Target setting, then, is concerned with: human resources; productivity and profitability; telling people what is expected of them, and providing a regular check on how they are getting on.

Suitable areas for target setting are:

- to set a standard of performance
- to raise a standard of performance
- to set new targets where existing ones have proved unrealistic
- to achieve something in particular
- to ensure that the manager's idea of the nature of the job is in line with the organisation's overall profit plan
- to innovate
- to develop the individual
- to cash in on unforeseen circumstances
- to implement a new policy.

Clarifying job objectives

The first essential is for you to be clear about the real objectives of your own job. This means you have to find out about the company's objectives and how your job relates to them. Only once you have done this will you be truly capable of clarifying to your subordinates the objectives of their jobs.

For example, the first step with your subordinates might be to see each of them singly and very briefly discuss with them your own job. Find out how much they know about your responsibilities, and fill in the gaps in their knowledge. By sharing information with them like this you'll make them feel ready to tackle the business of thinking through their jobs. Ask them to go away and jot down — on no more than a couple of sides of paper — the main responsibilities of their jobs. Then have a further talk with them, going over what they have written and discussing any points where your view of their jobs differs from theirs. There will almost certainly be some aspects whose importance you will feel the subordinates have exaggerated, and others which they may have completely failed to consider, so this sort of discussion can in itself be very valuable.

As a result of the discussion, the job can be set down in terms of an overall objective (a single short description, in not more than two or three sentences) plus about half a dozen key areas of responsibility together with an indication of expected standards of performance. The completed document is called a job description.

How this all works becomes immediately apparent when you look at an actual job description. Here, for example, are parts of a hypothetical one for a secretary:

Job title:	Secretary
Location:	Personnel Department
Responsible to:	Personnel Manager
Relationships:	Works in a department of six people: personnel officer, secretaries and clerks. Liases with all other departments — in particular, wages department, time office, medical department, training centre
Overall objective:	To assist the department manager by providing an efficient and responsible secretarial service.
Key areas:	1 To deal with correspondence 2 To arrange for and record proceedings of meetings 3 To maintain confidential files 4 To deal with telephone enquiries ... and so on.
Performance standards:	To deal with correspondence: 1(a) Receive and sort manager's mail: draw attention to urgent matters 1(b) Take down in shorthand and transcribe accurately all correspondence in accordance with house-style (minimum speeds: shorthand

90wpm, typing 50wpm)

1(c) Type letters, memos, reports, etc., by copying from manuscript or printed documents, to accepted standards of layout, accuracy, speed
... and so on.

To arrange for and record proceedings of meetings:

2(a) Fix date, time and place of meetings in accordance with manager's instructions

2(b) Prepare and sent out notices, agenda, minutes and other items not later than two clear days beforehand

2(c) Be in attendance at least 15 minutes before start of meetings to check final arrangements with manager.
... and so on.

You'll notice that the operation of producing a job description involves the individual in writing down the key areas (as he or she sees them) of the job. Responsibilities which can be described vaguely in speech take on a sharper meaning when one has to commit them to paper. When subordinates have to write out their 'draft job descriptions' they are already clarifying their jobs in their own minds.

Many managers feel that job descriptions are useless documents — as soon as they are written they go out of date, with the result that soon they are of no more than historical interest. This is indeed true of many job descriptions in the conventional form: they are just so much wasted paper.

To be of any use at all, a job description must be a dynamic document which is kept constantly up-to-date: far from being a dusty and neglected document, it should be a campaign plan. This can be achieved by distinguishing between the key areas and standards of a job, on the one hand, and the targets, on the other.

Standards of performance

A standard of performance is a continuing yardstick for judging acceptable performance. It should be realistic, be measurable in some way (quality, quantity, time or cost), and leave room for improvement. A subordinate should need no more than half a dozen simple standards of performance in each key area to demonstrate acceptable performance. From time to time you may see fit to check out some of the standards of performance — especially before a progress-review meeting.

At the departmental or sectional level, too, standards of performance are very necessary for effective functioning. Departmental standards require the joint efforts of a number of individuals within the team. Such team standards will not become a reality until individual department or section heads write personal standards of performance into their own job descriptions. There are many possible reasons why standards of performance might fail to be achieved: the job descriptions of the individuals in the team, from the manager downwards, may help pinpoint exactly what is wrong.

The targets

So, we're ready to consider those parts of a person's job which are subject to rapid change: his or her immediate targets. When we use the word 'target' we do not mean only production quotas or sales figures — in other words, things that can be counted and measured. A target is any short-term priority in the job, whether or not it can be quantified. For example, 'to improve relationships with the Sales Department' might be just as much a target for a manager as 'to reduce wastage by 4 per cent'.

In target setting there are five main questions which must be answered:

- how many?
- over what timescale?
- how easily achieved?
- how precise?
- how subject to change?

How many?

As we saw in Chapter 2, it is pointless to set too many targets. If more than about half a dozen targets are attempted in any one period, success in all of them is highly unlikely. The number of targets should provide a challenge, but should be realistic.

It is tempting to spread the targets equally across all of the key areas, so that each key area has, for example, a single target. Resist this temptation. The chances are that, at any one time, some objectives need to be emphasised more heavily than others. For example, an individual might have two targets dealing with customer relations and two dealing with future planning, with one target in each of the key areas of budget and interdepartmental relations. There might be no targets at all in the other key areas. Of course, this does not mean that these areas of the job should be neglected: remember, targets are priorities, special tasks to be achieved over and above the routine work.

Over what timescale?

Here, uniformity is not the key. A target such as 'establish regular meetings with the Sales Department' might take only a matter of weeks (or even days or hours) to achieve, whereas 'review the training needs of all chargehands in your division and arrange appropriate training for each of them' will take very much longer. Moreover, if all the targets have the same deadlines, subordinates are likely to run into difficulties. Besides, they must maintain the overall achievement of their job: the exercise is wasted if target setting destroys this.

How easily achieved?

On rare occasions a manager may want to set relatively easy targets for a subordinate whose confidence needs a boost, but in general there is little point in setting targets which do not call for an extra effort or an improvement in methods.

Arbitrarily imposing a difficult target on subordinates may make them feel that it is not even worth attempting — 'That's impossible!' — whereas, when subordinates are asked to suggest some targets themselves (subject to the manager's veto, of course), it is surprising how often they will propose a target more ambitious than the manager would have dreamt of setting.

Through participation in the target-setting process and the knowledge that they will be assessed against the targets, people's potential performance is greatly enhanced.

How precise?

The answer to this question is: precise enough to avoid argument as to whether or not the target has been achieved, but not so precise that they state the method by which the target is to be achieved. The managers should leave subordinates scope to exercise their initiative and to demonstrate their other abilities — such as drive, decisiveness, enthusiasm and leadership.

How subject to change?

When you and the subordinate set a target and fix a completion date you will act as seems best at the time, but conditions can change with bewildering speed. You should therefore agree at the outset to review the targets if need be before their planned completion dates — for example, if something more urgent crops up. Of course, a certain amount of commonsense has to be applied, since otherwise every minor shift in the wind will be taken as an excuse to extend the deadline.

Before setting targets you should ask yourself a few questions about the nature of the targets themselves. A typical 'mental questionnaire' might look something like this:

- how significant is this target in terms of the known aims and objectives of the organisation?
- how urgent is this target?
- to what extent is this target measurable, and what is the yardstick?
- how clearly is the target (especially the desired end result) described?
- to what extent is this target attainable?
- will the achievement of the target lead to a real end result, or is the target statement merely a description of an activity?
- to what extent will this target stretch the individual?

There are a few further points to consider when setting targets.

First, if it is not possible to allocate a proposed target to any of an individual's key areas, the chances are that it does not really form a part of the job at all.

Second, if you wish to apply target setting, do not wait for someone else to make the first move: set up the system in your own patch. In many cases, a pilot scheme instituted in one department has eventually led to the system being adopted throughout an organisation.

Third, there is no reason why target-setting schemes should be applied only to particular levels of management. Ideally, every manager of managers should be using such a system, from the very top of the organisation down to and including supervisor level.

Finally, it is sometimes said that target setting, while suitable for managers in, for example, production and sales, where tangible results are part and parcel of the job, cannot be applied to managers working in areas where achievements are 'intangible' — such as personnel and research. This is to take an unnecessarily narrow view, because targets need not always be quantitative. It may, however, make more sense for an organisation to establish a target-setting scheme in the more 'obvious' departments first, and then gradually extend the process into other areas.

Measuring performance against targets

If the initial impetus created by the progress of target setting is to be kept up, a system of progress reviews is needed.

At the time of establishing the first set of targets, you should fix a date three or four months ahead for a progress review. At this review, you should go over each target in turn to check whether or not it has been achieved. If it has been, both of you should try to see if anything can be learned from the methods used to achieve it.

If it has not been achieved, this may simply mean that the deadline was too optimistic, or that something more urgent has cropped up in the meantime. Otherwise, you should check if the lack of achievement was due to:

- failure on the subordinate's part (for example, leaving it too late)
- failure on your own part (for example, not allowing sufficient time or resources for the task to be performed)
- unforeseen circumstances (for example, sudden extra workload, or absence through sickness)

Each review gives both yourself and your subordinate the opportunity to discuss difficulties frankly, to identify the failing, and to agree the corrective action. This is constructive assessment, and opens the way to setting fresh targets for the next period.

As at the end of the initial interview, at the end of the progress review you should make a date for a further review in three or four months' time. This practice ensures that the intervals between reviews do not become longer and longer, until the whole process becomes murky and haphazard.

The annual appraisal interview — which should be a full-scale review of performance — therefore becomes part of a 'rolling process'. Any brief notes you have made at the progress meetings should be consulted. They will help to remind you of the trend of performance during the whole year's work, and will obviate the risk of your basing the appraisal meeting on only the results from the last few weeks.

The detailed design of the appraisal form you use will depend on your organisation's policy, number of staff, and so on, but certainly the following items should be included:

- your comments on performance, using both parts of the job description as your guide
- an estimate of suitability for promotion: to what type of post, and how soon
- comments on personal characteristics, but only insofar as they are relevant to the above two categories
- your plan for development by coaching, planned experience, training courses, etc.
- your subordinate's own views about their performance, and their future wishes
- a space for your own boss to concur or disagree with your comments, or to add any remarks.

There may be additional sections in the form, but these are the basics. It is worth stressing that the face-to-face discussion between yourself and your subordinate must take place before you complete the form.

Target setting as a tool

Target setting as a management tool has obvious value in the field of talent spotting for promotion. 'High fliers' or 'self starters' relish a system which gives them the chance to help set their own goals and at the same time to work towards the organisation's objectives. Indeed, it will be a test of your skill as a manager to bring such people on at the right pace, and if necessary hold them back from attempting targets out of their reach.

Certainly, once the setting of a target becomes generally adopted in an organisation, it puts a nail in the coffin of the 'blue-eyed boy' system of promotion. Comparing the performance records of different candidates is far more meaningful than trying to equate A's 'initiative — average' with B's 'cooperativeness — good'.

Target setting swiftly reveals training needs, and tends to aid greater delegation (see Chapter 5): in order to achieve their targets, managers may be more ready than they would otherwise be to delegate routine duties to their subordinates. Moreover, target setting is an adaptable technique: every manager knows that a task which would be shrugged off by one subordinate as simple will be a challenge to another (for a different target, it might be the other way round), so that managers must see that the chosen targets stretch people a little beyond their previous limit every time.

In essence, target setting is a simple and obvious procedure, but it should not be undertaken in the expectation that it will cure all of the organisation's problems overnight. What we can say is that those organisations which have introduced target setting have not only improved their efficiency but have also reaped enormous dividends in terms of higher morale, more meaningful assessment, reliable talent spotting, and, above all, improved performance in the job.

5 DELEGATION

If people are to give of their best at work, one crucial factor is letting them take their own decisions on how the job is to be done. In going for high performance, it is important that the right decision be taken, but it is also important that the decision is carried out with enthusiasm. The decisions which people carry out with most enthusiasm are the ones they have taken themselves — to the extent that, even if the decision was a wrong one, people will more often than not, through sheer effort, be able to turn it into a right one.

For this to come about, managers must learn to delegate. Deciding what parts of your job can be delegated, and then having the determination to carry it through, requires a great deal of conscious effort. It is not easy to give people the right to be wrong when you know that you are the person who will be held accountable for their mistakes. However, delegation is one of the single most important ways in which you can motivate the employees responsible to you — and that should more than compensate for any mistakes they might make.

Why is delegation important?

Delegation is not easy: it requires courage, patience and skill. Yet it is one of the most important aspects of our job, and one in which we frequently have great freedom of choice. For it is almost entirely at our own discretion what we choose to delegate, to whom, and at what stage.

Delegation is a lot more than just 'giving out work'. There are certain duties which fall naturally into the laps of subordinates, and with these the only action we may need to take is to decide which of our subordinates should be given a particular piece of work to do. But delegation is something different. Delegation can be defined as being when managers deliberately choose to give subordinates authority to carry out a piece of work which the managers could have decided to keep and carry out themselves.

Note the use of the word 'authority'. We must consider a few definitions, those of the words 'responsibility', 'authority' and 'accountability'. Responsibility, in this context, means the work that is delegated — the task, the job, the duty. Authority means the power or right to make decisions and take action to enable the responsibility to be successfully discharged. Accountability means carrying the can for the responsibility concerned — that is, being ultimately held to account for success or failure.

Successful delegation demands that we match responsibility with authority. To give someone responsibility without giving them equal authority is unreasonable and means that the venture is doomed to failure. A traffic warden without the power to issue tickets would have to be exceedingly persuasive to have any chance of preventing traffic obstructions. So we must always ensure that we give a subordinate an authority that is commensurate with the responsibility.

Accountability is a different matter. You are, ultimately, accountable for everything that goes on in your department. You can never shirk this: it is an integral part of your job. You cannot possibly make, or even know about, all the decisions taken but, in the words of Truman's famous notice, 'the buck stops here'. So, when you delegate, you do not shrug off your accountability — although how much you choose to delegate is of course up to you.

Delegation thus involves taking a calculated risk. But its advantages are such that if you ignore them you throw away a great opportunity.

First, delegation enables you to concentrate on those aspects of your job which require your personal experience, skill and knowledge — in other words, the aspects which mean that you 'earn your keep'. Contrast the occasions when you have felt 'What a footling day this has been — I've been wasting my time on trivia' with the occasions when you have felt tired but satisfied with the day's work, because you have been really stretched or because you know you have achieved something really tangible.

Second, much of your job should be concerned with planning the future rather than organising the present. If you are not planning ahead, you have to keep reacting to events rather than anticipating them, and your scope for initiative and enterprise is seriously limited. Delegation enables you to have the time to

49

look ahead, to anticipate problems, and to get one step ahead of your competitors.

Third, delegation does wonders for the morale of your employees. If we are good delegators, our departments are likely to experience lower absenteeism, less by way of office politics, more willingness to work late when the pressure is on, and so forth. Delegation motivates people, as we saw in Chapter 2. By contrast, if you are insular and secretive, and keep all decision taking to yourself, your subordinates will start becoming parochial and uncooperative, too.

Fourth, delegation is often the best of all possible ways of training your staff for greater responsibilities. When you need someone for an important task, or when a new opportunity crops up which you want to exploit, you are more likely to have the right person to hand if you have groomed your subordinates by constant delegation than if you are forced into the position of having to pitchfork someone suddenly into unfamiliar responsibility.

Finally, and quite selfishly, to delegate and watch your subordinates develop is perhaps the most satisfying experience you, as a manager, can have. Those are 'your' people, and you have helped them grow. You may lose some of them — perhaps to greater responsibilities in another part of the organisation, or perhaps to another organisation — but you are the one who has helped make their advancement possible.

The difficulties of delegation — and what can be done about them

We've looked at some of the major advantages of delegation, but it would be foolish to deny that there are also some difficulties. These are worth examining, because most of them prove not really to be difficulties but difficulties we find in ourselves when we have to adapt to the idea of delegation.

First, as we have already noted, delegation does involve risk. The first time we ask subordinates to carry out a new duty, we are probably more worried than the subordinates are. We are the person accountable: if they make a hash of it, we have to sort the whole mess out.

The only answer to the 'risk' problem is to accept it. Taking calculated risks is, after all, part of our job. We can, however, do much to minimise the risk (a) by planning the delegation carefully and (b) by showing subordinates that we have faith in their ability. Remember, confidence expressed is just as important as confidence felt.

The process of delegation is slow in the early stages, and inevitably there are setbacks. We must have patience, and not expect to see results immediately. Indeed, in the short term, you become busier than ever when you start delegating because you are taking on the coaching of your subordinates in addition to your normal workload.

Another difficulty about delegation is that it means we have to let go of certain duties which we enjoy doing, even if they are not central to getting the results that matter. The managing director of one organisation still keeps a large drawing-board in his office and spends several hours a week at it, tinkering around with designs. To a certain extent we all suffer from this. Those aspects of the job which we hate to let go of have been aptly named 'vocational hobbies'. We have to be tough with ourselves, and ration them down to not more than 5 per cent of our time. In fact, if they are kept at that level they can be very useful because, quite surprisingly often, our best ideas about important problems come when our minds are diverted from them. But remember, more than 5 per cent and we are flagrantly misusing our time.

Then there is the problem of daring to sit and think — which we certainly ought to have time to do if we have been delegating properly. The trouble is that, when we are engaged in constructive thought, we do not look busy. We have to accept the chance that one of our subordinates will catch us apparently just staring into space and will assume we are lazing: in fact, of course, we are probably busier than at any other time.

Some managers are reluctant to delegate because they want to feel 'on top of everything' and 'in touch with the work of the department'. They take all their important decisions themselves and require frequent detailed reports, checks and data from their subordinates. In fact, you will keep more truly 'in touch with the work of the department' through spot-checks and through regularly discussing progress and problems with your subordinates than by inspecting and approving all their work personally.

The most sensitive reason for reservations about delegating responsibility is the secret fear that our subordinates may outstrip us and gain promotion over our heads, or that by delegation we shall only accelerate the process of losing good people from our department. If your organisation has a good personnel policy, then you will be encouraged to develop your subordinates and may indeed see them being promoted into other departments — which should be a matter of personal satisfaction to you, as we noted earlier. Delegation — your delegation — will have helped them develop. If you do not delegate to worthwhile subordinates, on the other hand, you will lose them anyway, because they will become frustrated and leave to join another organisation. In the same context, it is worth delegating because, if the organisation thinks you are indispensable in your present job, they are less likely to promote you!

Perhaps the greatest reason for reluctance about delegation is the natural feeling that 'they won't do the job as well as I could'. In the early stages, this may very well be true: the first time you did something which is now second nature, how did you get on? No one should delegate recklessly but, if you have a subordinate who you think will do the job well enough, and who will quickly learn to do it well, then you should delegate without delay.

Of course, your subordinate may do that job in a different way from the way you would, but 'differently' does not always mean 'badly'. It is fascinating to see a subordinate tackle something new in a new way and — dare we say it? — occasionally get even better results than we would have.

What to delegate

To delegate properly you must have a plan. How should you go about this?

A good first step is to write down the main objectives of your job. If you already have a written job description (*see* Chapter 3), make sure it is up-to-date. By definition, 'main objectives' are not numerous and do not go into any great detail about means: they specify ends.

Next, go over your diary for the past month and note how you actually spent your time. Jot down roughly how long you spent each day on each activity, and compare the totals for the month. Even better, if you have a colleague with some work-study experience, get them to carry out a rough 'activity sampling' on you for a few days. This will reveal a pattern of what you actually do, under general headings such as 'attend meetings', 'incoming telephone calls' and 'discussion with subordinate (personal problem)'.

Armed with this information, draw up a simple chart comparing your objectives with your real-life activities. Note on the chart whether you think you are spending too much, too little or just about the right amount of time on each activity, and ask yourself to which of your objectives each activity contributes. Finally, you should list whether or not any activity could be delegated and, if the answer is 'yes', make some notes for action.

You are now ready to decide what can be delegated. Here there are some limitations on your choice. These must be recognised, and it is best to list those features of your responsibilities which cannot be delegated — even if you have a subordinate who is itching for more responsibility. Examples of the categories of responsibility which must stay yours are:

- tasks well beyond the skills and experience of your subordinates
- confidential, security and policy matters which are restricted to your own level of seniority
- matters involving the exercise of discipline over the subordinates' colleagues at their own level.

Do not use the fact that some responsibilities cannot be delegated as an excuse to rationalise your own reluctance to delegate.

Even after the list has been whittled down in this way, you will still have a range of possible tasks to delegate. The first two areas to look at are (a) routine tasks, and (b) tasks consuming a lot of your time.

Routine tasks are good material for delegation. What is routine to you will be new to your subordinate, and so by delegating it you will be both giving yourself more time to concentrate on the results you are being paid to achieve and stretching your subordinate's ability, thereby developing their personality.

Tasks that consume a lot of your time may well do so because you are not particularly good at them or because you have simply run out of new ways of tackling them. Your subordinate may be better at a task than you, and/or may come up with a better and quicker method. If you put the proposition to the subordinate like that these tasks become an irresistible challenge.

Training your subordinates in delegated tasks

Now that you have identified those tasks you wish to delegate, you have to consider how they should be passed on, and to whom. This can be done by privately analysing each of your subordinates in turn, thinking through these questions:

- what skills, qualifications and experience do they have (a) which are currently being used, and (b) which are not being used?
- what type of work have they shown an interest in but not as yet done?
- what type of work could they not do adequately even if given further training?

The answers to these questions should help you to decide which is the appropriate subordinate to take on each item of delegated responsibility, and draw up for each of them a delegation plan, as shown in the table.

You will want to discuss this with the subordinate concerned. If you are already operating a target-setting scheme (see Chapter 4) this discussion can conveniently take place at the time of a progress review.

In accepting a newly delegated responsibility, the subordinate must be clear about three constraints on the way it is handled: objectives, policies and limits of authority.

The way these constraints operate is best understood through an example. Imagine a departmental manager in an insurance company wishing to carry out a survey on claims against policies covering sickness while on holiday. She decides to delegate this task, which until now she has carried out herself, to a member of the department. She calls him in and briefs him as follows:

| Manager | "We need to take another look at our holiday sickness policies. You've seen the recent figures, and I'm not too happy about the trends. Now I'd like you to take on the responsibility for a survey covering the last three years." |
| Subordinate | "Well, I've never done a survey on my own before — how should I go about it?" |

Manager	"How you do it is very largely up to you. What I want you to be clear about are the objectives of the survey and the limits on your authority in carrying it out. I've dictated a note about this — let's look it over together. The objectives are: to carry out a survey on claims against UK holiday sickness policies over the past three years, in order on the one hand to compare our trends with those of our five leading competitors and, on the other, to produce recommendations for any changes in the premiums, together with estimates of the increased income and also possible fall-offs in sales of new policies and renewals as a result. You'll note that this survey extends only to holiday sickness claims in the UK — not holiday accidents, and not overseas. All right so far?"
Subordinate	"Yes, that's quite clear."
Manager	"Right. Now the limits: it shouldn't need more than three staff, including yourself; I would like your report by the end of the month; and the usual budget limitations apply. But for this project only you can have a contingency allowance of £250 for any travel you have to undertake during the survey."
Subordinate	"Will this survey follow the pattern of the one on accident claims on which I worked with you a few months ago?"
Manager	"I expect it to — but you go about it your own way. By the way, any ideas you can come up with about special premiums for young families would be welcome."
Subordinate	"Right. Actually, I've been thinking we might develop a clause about entire families holidaying together."
Manager	"That's the kind of thing. There's one other point I want to remind you about: company policy on surveys involving members of the public. Do remember to conform to that — the details are in your procedures manual."
Subordinate	"How will Mr Shipman in Accounts and Ms Parnell in the Legal Department know I'm going to be responsible for this?"

Manager   "Good point. I'm sending them a note — look, here's a copy. It makes it clear I've given you full authority for this project. Come back to me if you run into any problems — but since you've helped on a couple of other projects I think you'll find handling this one quite straightforward."

Notice that the manager has clearly explained the objectives of the task, spelt out the limits of the subordinate's authority, reminded him about company policy, and given him confidence and backing by notifying other departments and stressing her own availability if needed.

Many duties can be delegated progressively — indeed, very few can be handed over in their entirety in a single step. 'Gently does it' is the best approach in most cases. The diagram shows how the transition can be planned.

Once you have delegated a task, it is important that you notify all the other people who will be affected, especially those in other departments whose cooperation the subordinate may need. A brief note or a telephone call will be enough.

And, once the task has been completely handed over to the subordinate, make sure it is eliminated from your job description and written into theirs.

Statements of authority and responsibility

A written job description is a considerable aid to a manager so long as it is a constructive, up-to-date document and not, as so often happens, a dreary catalogue of limitations on initiative. Besides the job description, a booklet showing the extent of authority to take decisions can also be useful. As an example, British Insulated Callenders' Cables produced booklets called 'statements of responsibility and authority' (SRAs) for most of their middle management and supervisory staff. Part of the SRA booklet of a general superintendent, who had several foremen reporting to him, looked like this:

RESPONSIBILITY	AUTHORITY CODE		
	D	A	R
Requisition labour — replacement	●		
— additional			●
Arrange for employee whose work is below standard to have further training	●		
Lend or transfer employee outside superintendent's area of responsibility (making any necessary grade change)	●		
Authorise overtime: (a) for superintendents and foremen		●	
(b) to achieve production commitments — midweek	●		
— weekend			●
Issue warning in writing for disciplinary reasons	●		
Discharge employee for disciplinary reasons			●

* D = delegate, A = act, R = recommend

When SRAs are issued, the manager goes through them step by step with subordinates so that they understand them thoroughly, and in particular know whether any restrictions have been placed on their authority during the period of training.

Although SRAs can in the main deal only with 'predictable' that is, recurring decisions, they have been found to reduce substantially the uncertainty often experienced by supervisors, in particular, above been involved in drafting and using SRAs comment that they have served to clarify 'grey' areas and speed decision making. Also, the effect of SRAs on delegation has been considerable, and they have clearly highlighted training needs. In practice, the system can be developed and adapted by shifting the cross into a different column as the job-holder becomes more experienced. That is, the newly appointed supervisor is likely to have a lot of crosses in the 'R' column, but as time goes on many of these will be moved into the 'A' column and some into the 'D' column.

Just as with an appraisal scheme, any system like the SRA one should be checked at least annually to see what opportunities there are to push decision making further down the line. The annual appraisal interview is a good time to do this.

Mistakes, and how to handle them

However careful you have been, inevitably sometimes a subordinate will make a mistake in a delegated task. How should you handle such a situation?

Your approach should depend on the reason for the mistake.

If, for example, the subordinate omitted to consult somebody and irritated that person as a result, you should check whether you made it sufficiently clear at the outset who was to be consulted. If you did not, you should do the apologising — both to the person concerned and to your subordinate. If, on the other hand, you did make it clear but the subordinate overlooked it, then it is the subordinate who must make his or her peace with the offended party. You will want to remind your subordinate, from your experience as a manager, how crucial interdepartmental cooperation is.

If subordinates abuse their newly acquired authority, you should point out that delegation is a trust, and that you want to have confidence that it is not abused.

The subordinate may make a mess of a job through lack of planning. Probably, you should give a little patient coaching. It may be, the subordinate thought, from having seen you do the task, that there was nothing to it. You need to demonstrate that what you can now do in a flash originally required considerable care and preparation.

Sometimes a task grinds to a halt for no apparent reason. This may be because the subordinate lacks confidence. Talk it over carefully, and try to find out what it is that is causing the subordinate difficulty. Perhaps they are not good at figurework? Or is it that the subordinate has to chair meetings, and has never done this before? Whatever the reason, you may have to go back to the previous stage in the process of coaching and build up their confidence by slow degrees.

More seriously, the subordinate just may not measure up to the new responsibility. You will then have to judge if the subordinate could do it with more training, or if you should cut your losses and go through the ticklish process of taking the task back or giving it to another subordinate (which requires even more tact).

Throughout this process of analysing mistakes, it is helpful to keep two points at the forefront of your mind. First, everyone makes mistakes at some stage and, as long as they are not caused by sheer foolhardiness, there is little to be ashamed of. Second, as the cliché has it, people can learn from their mistakes. You can use a subordinate's failures as a platform for coaching.

Even if no mistakes are being made, you still have a responsibility for control. The simplest method to use is perhaps the spot check. After the subordinate has carried out the task a couple of times, you can check how it is going. If the task involves much liaison with another department, have a quiet word with the departmental head to see how they think your subordinate is handling things. If the task involves written work, ask your subordinate for a copy of the report concerned. If it involves running a committee, have a word with one of the committee members.

But do all these things only occasionally. Spot checks can easily turn into regular reports, and the subordinate will soon feel you have delegated with one hand while keeping a firm grip with the other. In particular, if your feedback on their performance is favourable, do let the subordinate know this. 'Congratulation is the lost art of management', as someone once said. A job being well done deserves recognition, and a word of praise is a powerful motivating force.

Evaluating the results of delegation is likewise often overlooked. You can learn a lot if a task has been successfully delegated. Questions to pursue include:

- has the subordinate found a new way of performing the task which could be copied elsewhere?
- is the subordinate capable of still further development?
- are there other tasks currently handled by yourself which you could now delegate?
- has the subordinate's success stimulated others of your team to seek more responsibility?
- has the subordinate's experience told you anything about the training period necessary to perform this sort of task?
- can you improve your own coaching ability, so that in future it will be easier to delegate tasks?
- how much of your time has been saved, and how are you using it?

This last question is especially pertinent. Once you have delegated a task it is easy to let the time saved be eaten away again, and you may end up with the disgruntled feeling that delegation does not pay. Evaluating the results of delegation will ensure that it does pay, and will help you see how to make it pay still more.

Management by exception

Once the task really belongs to the subordinate and you have the confidence to let them get on with it, once you have carried out a few spot checks and an evaluation, what next? Well, then you should be able to rely on management by exception.

We have all seen managers' desks piled high with detailed reports of every single minutia concerning what is going on in their departments. By ploughing through these reports every day, managers can get an extremely accurate picture of what is going on in their department. However, one shudders to think of all the things managers are not doing while they are painstakingly analysing all this stuff.

Management by exception is the exact opposite. You assume that the accepted standards are being met unless you are told otherwise: no news is good news. You are not bothered by masses of paperwork. Such reports as you do get highlight deviations from the normal. You can concentrate your attention on the deviations, rectify those that are deviations for the worse and congratulate those responsible if they are for the better, rather than having to unearth them among long columns of figures.

Of course, you cannot manage entirely by exception. Apart from anything else, it becomes rather demoralising if the only reports you receive are of things going wrong. But a great many aspects of most managers' jobs could be handled in this way. Standards are set, those responsible get on with their delegated jobs, and you get quick feedback when things start to go out of line. It is like the difference between management accounting — where only the crucial figures are presented as the basis for managerial decisions — and traditional, 'archaeological' accounting — where the past is dug up, mistakes are raked over, endless post mortems are held, and aeons of management time are wasted.

In many organisations time and effort are spent on checks and controls, and far less time is spent on reviewing the very standards that generate such checks. However, if such reviews are carried out on our present standards, we produce more realistic standards and management by exception then really comes into its own.

Delegation, as we have seen, is not easy. Rather like abstract concepts such as peace and justice, everyone is in favour of it until they start to realise how much effort is needed for its achievement. Above all, it requires honesty — to assess how we are using our time, and, once we have embarked on a delegation plan, perseverance in the face of the inevitable discouragements.

However, the manager who fails to delegate is no real manager. The manager who delgates well has at least made a start.

6 DECISION TAKING

Whether you like it or not, you are going to get nowhere without the committed enthusiasm of your subordinates, and nowhere is this more true than in the field of decision taking. Managers can decide what they think needs to be done, but making it happen is another thing entirely. How often have you heard a manager say something like 'It's not taking decisions that's so difficult — the hard part is getting people to go along with them and help make them work'?

Leadership, motivation, delegation — all of these things play their part in helping your decisions be brought into effect by the cooperative actions of your subordinates.

The decisions you have to take

Cutting down on costs is a difficult job, but it is one which we must often face. However, the difficult part is not really the mathematical exercise: what really gives us ulcers is working out how the proposed cost savings are going to be implemented, because this means upsetting the very people whose support we need. The same is true of so many other regular managerial tasks. Of course, we can take the attitude that 'you can't have a good salary and a round of applause'; and naturally there is no magic formula — no sort of on/off switch for instant management — that will solve the problem. But at the same time there are some principles we can observe if we want to make our lives — as well as the lives of those whom our decisions affect — a little easier.

What sort of decisions are we talking about? It would be impossible within this short chapter to cover every possible eventuality. However, we can consider the various courses of action open to you when you take decisions which affect people or groups of people operating in a normal working environment. Such decisions fall into three main categories:

- decisions which are predictable and obvious, and which cause comparatively little dissent, if any
- decisions which have to be taken in sudden emergencies, when consultation is not possible
- the others

In the third category come those decisions which are reached after a lot of careful thought, those which do not work unless they are consulted upon, taken more quickly, properly briefed, or monitored carefully; decisions which affect people and the way in which they work. Most of all, decisions which our organisation pays us to take and to implement in the most committed and efficient way we can.

But the important factor in taking and implementing decisions is the human one. You simply cannot afford to make assumptions about the effects of decisions upon people. Almost every decision affects your subordinates — and their subordinates, and so on down the line — in a direct or indirect way. People can be remarkably flexible in their responses to the effects of your decisions — just so long as they are told about them and told why.

For example, a few years ago an engineering company decided to experiment with some new, numerically controlled, machines in the toolroom. The unions were consulted, and they agreed without demur to the experiment taking place. However, nobody bothered to communicate the decision or the reasons for it to the workforce. When the employees returned to work after the summer shut-down, they took one look at the machines and walked straight out again. However much management and the unions protested that the machines were only there as an experiment, the workforce — quite naturally — believed that there was something underhand going on because nobody had given them any warning or explanation. An unnecessary dispute had broken out because of failure to communicate.

It is our object, as action-centred leaders, to make sure this sort of thing does not happen to us.

Taking and implementing decisions: a framework

Soundings taken among a number of managers have given us a way of constructing a sort of basic framework for the process of taking and implementing decisions. Of course, in the real world, no situation will conform exactly to the framework; but almost every situation can be expected to match it approximately.

Decision taking has to be approached in a systematic way in order to promote greater consistency and efficiency, and this the framework allows. Its basis is that, in any situation where a decision must be taken and implemented, there are five actions managers need to take — the five Cs: consider, consult, crunch, communicate, and check. Of course, at any particular time, you will be involved in more than one of the Cs — you may be communicating, for example, long before you have finished consulting — but it is useful and revealing to break down the complex process in this way.

Using the framework

However many stages there are to a decision, it is first vital to be clear as to who should take it. Here delegation is the key. All managers are more enthusiastic about implementing a decision they have taken themselves, and so it makes a great deal of sense to delegate a decision as far down the line as possible. As we saw in Chapter 5, this can be difficult, because you have to trust people and be prepared to carry the can for any subordinates who make mistakes, as, from time to time, they inevitably will. However, it is better to take the risk of delegating decision taking and enjoy all the boons of a motivated staff than it is to keep everything to yourself.

Motivation is again a question when it comes to considering group decisions. Group decisions are frequently an outward and visible sign of consensus and compromise, which means that few people feel any real enthusiasm for them (unless the decision is obvious). Also, they're frequently a result of the majority having outvoted the minority, so that the latter have no real interest in the decision. Nobody remains accountable for what happens, so that if queries or problems arise people feel free to pass the buck

— hence the 'don't blame me, chum — I didn't want it' attitude.

In determining who should be the person responsible for taking the decision, ask yourself these three questions:

- who is likely to be the person most committed to making the decision work?
- should it be delegated?
- has the subordinate you are considering got sufficient authority and knowledge?

Just before we consider the use of our framework in terms of the five Cs, it is worth noting a possible pitfall. Because decisions frequently affect an entire group of people, some managers are tempted to implement decisions because they will be popularly received by the group even though they may not necessarily be the right course of action. Don't be afraid of making an unpopular decision — so long as there is not a good reason for its being so unpopular.

Consider

The decision-taking process starts as soon as it becomes apparent that some management action or initiative is necessary. The first need is to make sure that the real problem is to be tackled and not merely the superficial symptoms of some underlying — possibly organisation-wide — failure. The second need is to ensure that intervention is in fact necessary: some problems can solve themselves without the need for outside help. Sometimes, although the present situation is far from ideal, any probable option is likely to be even worse. In both such circumstances the best possible decision a manager can take is to take no decision.

It is important to spend some time considering what your aim is — what it is that you want to achieve. Also, you will probably need to review a fair amount of information before you can make your mind up; it is worth spending some preliminary time deciding what information you need, and where you can get it.

You must clarify the constraints within which action must be taken. Company restraints, in the form of company policy and precedent, legal constraints and financial constraints will obviously influence your decision, as will the views of any trade unions involved. However, the constraint which will require you to think hardest will probably be time. What is the latest time by which the decision must be taken? If you decide too soon you may be depriving yourself of relevant information which has as yet not come to light, or time to consider other factors which might influence your thinking. But, on the other hand, if you delay too long you may just see the problem getting worse, or you may prevent others in the organisation from getting on with their jobs, thereby wasting resources.

Consult

As we have noted, experience has shown that group decision making is generally to be avoided, for a number of reasons. Yet at the same time all the evidence is that, when people are not involved in decisions that affect them, it is hard to obtain their commitment. The most effective way of involving people is to adopt the process of consultation before decision. The crucial word here is the middle one — 'before'. Consulting people after decisions have been made is rarely productive and not infrequently leads to resentment — as many managers have found out to their cost. The exceptions to this principle are when (a) time simply does not permit it, or (b) the decision concerns commercial confidentiality and therefore cannot be taken openly. In cases like this, it is vital that a full explanation is given afterwards of why consultation was impossible. Otherwise you're asking for trouble.

It cannot be stressed too often that a manager works through people, and so you must ensure that you carry those people with you. But people perceive facts and situations from different viewpoints. They see things differently from the way you do, their feelings are involved, their interests are affected, their jobs and security may appear to be threatened and, above all, they often have considerable knowledge and experience as a result of having themselves to take decisions and do the actual work. They may not in fact want to take your decision for you, but they have a right to be involved in the decision-taking process.

Consultation may in many instances be limited to the immediate work group and this is often the case with operational decisions. However, some tactical and strategic decisions affect far wider areas of an organisation, and such instances call for the use of whatever formal consultation arrangements may exist. The organisation may or may not be unionised: if unions are recognised they must of course be included in the consultation.

Whenever consultation is in progress, the maximum amount of information should be made available to all concerned.

The timing of consultation will often call for sensitivity and judgement. There is a strong case to be made for consulting as early as is practicable so as to allow as much time as possible to weigh up the pros and cons of the situation. On the other hand, the desirability of early consultation has to be weighed against the need to avoid long-drawn-out and possibly destructive discussion of contentious issues, not to mention the likelihood of raising hopes or apprehensions unnecessarily early.

Whenever you choose to start consultation, it is wise to set a time limit, so that everyone knows when the consultation will have to stop so that the decision can be taken.

Crunch

Once you are certain that you have satisfied all the initial stages, you should set yourself a deadline by which you will make up your mind. Once this deadline is reached, you must decide. You may well find yourself looking for excuses to put off the dreaded moment (perhaps more information will become available?) but you should ignore the temptation. Far better instead to:

- review the information you may already have, which should include feelings as well as facts
- try to assess the extent to which the absence of some information will affect the quality of the decision
- list the options and the arguments for and against
- decide what you have to decide.

On occasion the option you have decided upon can be described not so much as the 'best' but as the 'least worst', since almost certainly, in any decision, there will be some disadvantages and some interests will be adversely affected. For this reason, you may require courage and resolution in the face of unpopularity and dissent.

Communicate

More good decisions founder because of poor communication than for any other single reason. You have probably seen this happen yourself. So, how do you get the communications right?

The only way to put a decision over to people and secure their commitment is to do it face-to-face, so that they can have the chance to ask questions. You are engaged in what is essentially a selling operation, and this will fail if its only aid is a notice on the board or an announcement in the company newsletter.

Remember, too, that it is the job of whoever takes the decision to ensure that it is communicated to all concerned. By definition, therefore, sole reliance on union and staff representatives to get your message across is inadequate. Union and staff representatives are there to represent the workforce to the management, not to sell management's decisions to the workforce. They may agree to help, but you cannot expect them to. After all, it is not their job — it's yours.

The real question is: what exactly should you be communicating? The crucial elements are, as we have seen, the decision and the reasons for it. It is also vital to supply a few practical examples, so that the message is made 'real' to its receivers. People need to understand when the decision will be implemented, who will be affected (and how), and what the procedure is for registering a complaint or grievance.

Many communication problems can be overcome by the use of team briefing to ensure that the decision and the reasons for it go right the way down to those it affects. This system guarantees also that the message is put over only by those who can be accountable for having done so, so that managers can check that even an unpopular decision is correctly and enthusiastically put over — and it is enthusiasm that provides the springboard for a decision's success. If your subordinates are doing their job properly — and of course you should insist they do — they'll put the message over and not be tempted to fall back on weak apologies of the 'it's not my fault, it was management's decision' type.

Team briefing is a good way of making sure that managers actually manage, and that they are reinforced and consolidated in their rightful positions as leaders of the work group.

Check

Finally, you need to know if the decision you have taken is actually working. Naturally, a great deal of information can be obtained through the normal channels of returns and statistics, not to mention the feedback from union and staff representatives and from briefing groups. However, there is no substitute for going out to see for yourself. By walking the job (see Chapter 1) you can observe the effects of your decision by being on the spot and talking with people — listening not just to what they say but also to the way they say it. Moreover, and importantly, observing for yourself enables you to determine whether or not any corrective action is necessary. And, above all, it allows your subordinates to see that you are acknowledging your own responsibility.

If the decision is working, fine, although it is worth expending a little thought on the reasons for your success — that'll help you make an equally good decision next time. But what if it isn't? When you are trying to find out the reasons for the failure of a decision, you might like to ask yourself the following questions — was it due to any of these?

- inadequate information
- poor judgement
- lack of courage
- inadequate plans for implementation
- bad communication
- a lack of enthusiasm on the part of management
- change of circumstances between decision and implementation.

Decision taking and participation

We live in a participative age, one in which people expect a great deal more from their work than did previous generations. One of our problems today is that many managers understand only too well at one level that nowadays they manage by consent, but simultaneously, at another level, refuse to accept this reality. So, in the knowledge that a decision is likely to be resisted — perhaps actively — they attempt to impose it. The consequences are obvious.

To be successful today, we have to be willing to adopt a much more open style of management, and to take the initiative to ensure that the people in our workforce understand both the aims of the organisation and their own individual role within it. Somehow, we have to create an environment which encourages people to make use of their resources and their ingenuity. Therefore the objectives and policies of the section, department, company or even group ought to be the subject of joint discussion among those people who are involved in implementing them and achieving results.

This bothers some managers. They worry that if they involve people more in the decision-taking process they will become redundant themselves, or lose their authority or status. Such managers have to be convinced that, on the contrary, increasing the involvement of their subordinates places greater demand on managers' skills and abilities — not less. True, the very skills and abilities managers require in the modern participatory style of management may require development, either through training or simply by carrying out the right actions, but this is far from impossible.

Of course, managers today still take decisions, but they do it very differently from the old style of simply dictating to their subordinates what was to be done. While a few managers bemoan this fact, most recognise that participating employees are motivated employees (see Chapter 2) and that those employees may very often have something useful to contribute to the discussion, perhaps causing the planned decision to be amended or even demonstrating to management that the best decision is to make no decision at all.

A classic example of the benefits of participation took place a few years ago in a company which was very keen to make some alterations to its internal structure in order to sharpen up its selling/marketing potential. However, in order to implement the change, the chief executive planned to move a number of employees from one part of the company to another. He consulted these employees, and was so impressed by the level of opposition to his plans that he used his judgement and took a decision then and there to leave matters as they were. However, he also gave his reasons for wanting to make the changes, and invited constructive suggestions as to how they could be brought about. On the basis of the suggestions he received he was soon able to make changes which met his objective without any opposition at all.

A number of companies have issued decision-taking policies for managers' guidance. These differ markedly in form, but comparatively little in substance. The key points — and the key points in this chapter — are:

- delegate the decision as far down the line as practicable
- do suffcent preparation, perhaps using specialists, to make discussions with employees or their representatives meaningful

- consult those who are likely to be affected
- explain why you have taken the decision
- be consistent in the management approach to the decision: the leaders at each level must see that it is implemented energetically, whether or not they personally agree with it
- consult those who are likely to be affected
- explain why you have taken the decision
- be consistent in the management approach to the decision: the leaders at each level must see that it is implemented energetically, whether or not they personally agree with it
- the overall guiding principle in decision taking is furtherance of the organisation's objectives
- if events show the decision to have been wrong, you must be prepared to admit you have made a mistake and change the decision if necessary
- people have a right of appeal: if someone believes that the decision is unjust and not merely a difference of opinion, they must be encouraged to make use of the grievance procedure or, after talking to the immediate boss, go to the level above to state their case.

7 EFFECTIVE USE OF TIME

Shortage of time is often used by managers to explain delays and failures and as an excuse for inefficiency and lack of forethought. True, some of us really do suffer from lack of time, but in almost every case there are things we ought to be able to do to remedy the problem. In addition to our other duties as managers, we must learn to manage time.

Proper management of time is crucial to the success of British industries and institutions, yet so many of us find that our time is taken up by coping with paperwork, sitting on the telephone, dealing with interruptions, making snap decisions on trivial matters because they're urgent, trying to work late into the night . . .

In this chapter we look at various ways of creating time for ourselves so that we are able to do all the things our organisation pays us to do. We shall start with one that is all too often forgotten: thinking.

Thinking

There is a strong instinctive feeling that we have to look 'busy' all the time — or at least when the boss is around. The idea of taking 'time off' to stop and think produces qualms. Yet thinking must be a central part of any work if it is going to be productive. To do it properly calls for concentration, self-discipline and proper allocation of time for the purpose. For example, a senior official of one professional institute advises members to set aside a certain period each day purely for thinking — and he sets an example by himself endeavouring to keep the hours between 3pm and 5pm every afternoon free for exactly that. He is earning his salary because he is thinking about how his group can better contribute to the organisation — exactly what he is being paid to achieve.

The tale is told of an employee in a US company who was

pestering his boss for a pay-rise. 'Look at So-and-so,' said the 'busy busy' employee. 'He gets twice the pay that I do, yet all he does is sit and look out of the window all day.'

'Well,' replied the boss, 'if you could think the thoughts that he's thinking . . .'

Not all thinking need be directed at solving work problems. The brain needs frequent, short 'concentration breaks', and we can use the day's inevitable hold-ups for these. Neither should we insist that we stop thinking once we have found a solution to our particular problem — letting the mind freewheel for a while is a source of great pleasure. And why shouldn't we indulge ourselves? If an hour's worth of concentrated thinking can reduce by an hour the time it takes to achieve a task, then surely we can have half an hour's 'play thinking'? The organisation is still profiting from the time we've spent in thought.

Our brains are much more efficient than we often realise. The brain of an infant develops at a pace far outstripping anything that the hi-tech computer scientists even dream about. But the brain needs regular exercise to attain a high level of efficiency, just like an athlete needs regular training in order to do well in a race. So time spent in 'play thinking' is far from wasted: it is the brain's 'training'.

We think a lot faster than we talk. Few people can speak more than about 200 words per minute, yet most of us habitually think at more than 600 words per minute (in fact, the difference can be thousands of times greater, because we often think in concepts rather than words), which suggests that we can gain an advantage by doing more listening and less interrupting! The time saved can be put to good use — we can think about a range of options, rather than relying on instinct to select the right one immediately.

When we are thinking about work problems we tend to opt for what is called analytical thinking, where logical deduction from known facts leads to a more or less indisputable answer. Most of us are good at this — it is the way we were taught. But there are times when we need creative thinking, when we have to bring the imagination into play because, from the known facts, logical deduction yields more than one answer — or no answer at all.

Creative thinking needs adjusting to. When we first try it we find ourselves hitting barriers. Self-imposed limits get in the way of new ideas. We stick to the belief that there is always only one right answer, or we don't want to look foolish, or we want to conform, or we don't make the effort to look at the 'obvious' and see if it really is all that obvious.

Creative thinking relates things or ideas that were not previously related — indeed, it is rather like 'play thinking'. Thoughts proceed on one plane and then suddenly veer off in a new direction. The resulting release of tension often makes us burst out laughing (joke writers use this technique a lot).

A successful business thrives on creative thinking. It can stay ahead of the competition with better marketing, improved products and services, and higher motivation. For example, a well known pen manufacturer once suddenly improved their own performance and altered the shape and size of the whole marketplace simply because someone there suddenly realised the company was in the 'gift' business.

Brainstorming employs creative thinking to produce lots of ideas quickly. To get the best results, call together a small group of amenable people for about half an hour. Someone among you should be able to write the ideas down very quickly — and legibly. Pose the questions and then encourage a flood of ideas. Once the stream has dried up, stop and gaze silently at the chart(s). Allow the ideas to incubate until someone begins to see the 'last piece of the jigsaw' — this is known as the AHA! moment. Sometimes even the silliest notion can be pulled inside-out to give you yet another useful idea.

The keys to successful brainstorming are:

- getting the problem, the statement of the question, right in the first place
- consciously and deliberately separating the production of ideas from their evaluation
- letting people whose temperament or mood do not fit the occasion slip away without loss of face
- agreeing that no one will feel humiliated if they produce a really silly idea.

For private thinking, on the other hand, there is no need for a separate office or for a secretary to repel possible interruptions. Many people simply avert their gaze from approaching visitors, put up a hand, or turn away for a moment. A good train of thought, once disturbed, is hard to recapture. People respect our need for five seconds' grace.

Last, remember not to try to think too hard. We have all had the experience of desperately trying to think of something without success, and then later finding that the answer pops into our head. If the answer to a problem won't come, let your mind freewheel for a while. Chances are you'll find the solution.

Decisions

In Chapter 6 we looked at the process of decision taking in some detail. However, there are many routine decisions we make which affect only a few people around us — or perhaps even affect only ourselves. What are the most time-effective ways of making these 'small-scale' decisions?

It is helpful to go to the trouble of writing down what it is we are trying to achieve — in other words, a statement of the problem. In practice, we rarely do this because we assume we already know what is wanted. However, putting things down on paper has a powerful effect on the clarity of our thoughts. Often what seemed to be the central problem turns out to be merely a symptom of something else.

Once we are satisfied we have got the problem right, and when we have defined our objective, we are ready for some concentrated thinking. At this stage we generate several possible solutions and try to predict the probable outcome of each. Now comes the time to decide and act: we choose and implement the most appropriate plan. If necessary, we should share it with other people, and later we should check periodically to see how it is working out in practice.

Although the consultation may be with ourselves alone, we are really going through the five Cs (*see* page 65).

Telecommunications

Here are two sets of dialogue representing the sorts of telephone conversations you hear several times daily in organisations all over the country:

Dialogue A

Brring, brring!
   'Mr Jones's office.'
   'Can I speak to him, please?'

'I'm afraid he's not in.'
'Do you know when he'll be back?'
'No, I'm awfully sorry, I don't. Can I take a message?'
'Er ... no, it's all right. I'll ring again later on.'

What has been achieved? Nothing. A recent survey produced the depressing result that 60 per cent of telephone calls failed to produce the wanted information on the first attempt. Moreover, less than one person in ten who promised to ring back actually did so.

With proper training and good leadership a subordinate can choose to handle such a call quite differently:

Dialogue B

Brring, brring!
'Production. Jim Watts speaking.' (The voice ends on an upward note.)
'Ah, Bill Ferris here from Bradley and Stokes. Is Freda Jones in?'
'Not at the moment. We're expecting her back between three and three-thirty this afternoon. Is it something I can help with, Mr Ferris?'
'Well, yes, I'm sure you could ...'

By using our own names in this way we encourage callers to give their names, too. (This saves the awkward 'Who's calling?', especially if the person on the other end thinks we ought to recognise their voice.) Now that we know who we are speaking to we can decide how to proceed; for example, we know how much information we ought to divulge, or whether, perhaps, we should tell the caller bad news but in a positive way. We have organised a time-band during which Ms Jones will be available to take and make phone calls. And, since 'god' is away, the caller might just as well parley with one of the angels.

If you happen to be Freda Jones, Jim Watts has just saved some of your time — which is a good thing. Moreover, giving people every chance to work independently rather than in someone else's shadow is always a good thing, as we saw over and over again in Chapter 5.

One national company has a policy whereby people deal completely with a telephone enquiry even if it has come through to the wrong department. Staff listen carefully, write down the question, read it back to the caller and promise action within a specified deadline. Once the call is over, find out which department is the correct one and pass the message on with due urgency. No more transferring callers from one department to another means less annoyance and a better service. The caller's time has been saved, and so, on average, has the company's.

When you are making rather than receiving a call there are a few simple rules which can help save both time and money:

- decide who to contact, and think of an alternative should they be out
- have the number, dialling code and extension/department written out in front of you
- make brief notes of what you plan to say or ask
- get together any papers you may need to refer to
- make the call, but never let the ringing tone sound more than five times
- on reaching the person you want, state who you are, clearly explain the general purpose of the call, give the message or ask the question, and then check that the person has understood you
- if you cannot get the person at once, do not hold on: offer to ring back after an agreed interval
- ring back when you said you would.

Such a drill can be used by organisations to halve the overall costs of long-distance telephone calls — not least by cutting out long and expensive silences. When tariffs are lower in the afternoons, use the telephone as little as possible in the mornings.

A word about telephone operators. They have an unusual job which ought to be sympathetically understood by all extension users. The pressures of the job vary between having nothing to do and being rushed off one's feet. Everyone can help the telephonist if they just spend a moment or two thinking about what life is like at the console.

Technology

The average office today contains a number of hi-tech machines which can save you time. Among these are teleprinters and fax machines, computers and word processors. Fax machines are the most useful — replicas of your letters can be sent within minutes to any part of the world — but at the same time they are the most expensive. Teleprinters do roughly the same job, but are fading from use because fax machines are better at it. Computers are overused in modern offices: often people spend more time doing things on a computer than they would if they were doing the things on paper. However, computers can be very useful for things like keeping accounts. Word processors can save a lot of time; for example, this book was written on a word processor, and typeset directly from the discs produced by the machine, thereby saving both typesetting time and proofreading time. However, word processors can actually waste time if people use them only as glorified typewriters: training (*see* Chapter 9) is essential if people are to use word processors correctly.

Paperwork

The best advice is: get rid of the stuff as soon as you can!

The legal adviser in one transport company has a drawer in her desk labelled TDTDWT, meaning 'too difficult to deal with today'. A busy department head in a registered charity has a tray called GROAN — 'get rid of, anywhere, now'! And another manager keeps a big OBE file where he collects things he knows will be 'overtaken by events'.

One good question in connection with paperwork is: 'Why do I have to deal with it all?' The answer is that you probably don't: many of the tasks which engender all this paper could probably be delegated to your subordinates (*see* Chapter 5 for a full discussion) thereby spreading the responsibility and also the load of letters, forms, memoranda, bulletins and so on.

One way of tackling incoming paperwork is to sort each piece of paper into one of the following categories:

- immediate action can be taken: do what is called for, make a note in the margin, and then into the out-tray with it
- action can be started but not completed: do what you can and make a note in the margin
- items for information, reading and/or circulation.

If an incoming piece of paperwork in this last category is short you can read it immediately and get rid of it. The 'heavier' items can be gathered together and gone through during a daily 'reading time'. Do not sit on a circulation item: if you cannot finish with it in 24 hours, pass it on with a note requesting it be sent back to you after everyone else on the list has seen it. Throw away any item you don't need to keep.

Many replies can be written directly onto incoming memos, which can then be sent straight back. If you need a record, take a photocopy — a lot less expensive and time-consuming than sending a typewritten memo in reply. Also, you can photocopy a supply of 'reply notes' and clip them onto incoming memos: a few handwritten words and the job is done (see diagram).

Meetings

Meetings and committees are widely regarded as prime time-wasters. But, if they are well planned and run, they can be the best (even the only) way to brief staff on policy, progress and points for action; to uncover facts; to produce new ideas, and to get people involved and motivated (see Chapter 2).

This is neither the time nor the place to go into all the techniques whereby meetings can be made both briefer and more useful, but we can note that there are two main elements in any meeting: the person in the chair and the participants. Courses are available in the art of chairing meetings, but in essence the art is in the deft use of questions to stimulate discussion, keep to the point, summarise, tactfully reject irrelevances, and encourage shy people to contribute.

By the law of averages, you will be more often a participant than a chairperson. If you want to be a useful member of the meeting and get the best out of it, you will not allow emotions, interdepartmental battles or office politics to inject unwanted 'hidden agendas' into the discussion. Also, you will be:

- knowledgeable on the subject matter, aware of the purpose of the meeting, interested, and conscientious (especially about advance preparation)
- seated in place on time, and equipped with the requisite papers and materials
- prepared to air your views strongly, to make out a good case, to keep to the point, to listen to other opinions, and to be influenced by reason
- disciplined and patient, and prepared to contribute your best thinking and experience concisely and at appropriate times

- prepared to accept whatever decision is reached, to defer to the control of the chair, and to carry through on schedule any action assigned to you

Needless to say, ideally you should also be able to produce new ideas, help to refine and develop other people's ideas, listen, help to keep the discussion to the point, and, where necessary, ask for clarification and summaries.

Other people's time

Middle managers spend about half their time on unplanned and quite brief items, lasting from about 45 seconds to five minutes: contacts, queries, confirmations, progress check-ups, and so on. All the rest has to be fitted into the other half of the day. However, the impromptu encounters are not unnecessary and are not just useless interruptions. They are essential contacts without which the people on the shop floor are unable to get on with their jobs. Moreover, such contacts help us know what is really going on.

For example, a few years ago a leading group of builders' merchants wanted to install a new set of staff schemes, and therefore set about analysing what the employees' various jobs were. Some of the managers were astonished at how little they knew of what people actually did. The overlap between the job description written by one of the employees and the version written by his manager was less than one third. The ensuing discussion brought new insight. The office was shifted around. A direct-line telephone was put on the employee's desk, thereby saving him a great deal of time. He got his own copies of professional journals, rather than being 'permitted' to keep any that survived the rigours of a long circulation list. Efficiency improved overnight.

Our actions — or inactions — can have a further-reaching effect than often we may like to admit. Inept delegation, where all we are trying to do is to solve our own time problems by shuffling them off onto other people, is clearly self-defeating: all we are doing is making their lives more difficult, not solving any problem at all. Indeed, most of us have been guilty, at one time or another, of getting in other people's way. Here are a few things to avoid — although you should bear in mind that, occasionally, committing one of these 'sins' is in fact the right thing to do:

- simply transmitting information instead of 'sharing' it
- keeping people waiting unnecessarily
- interrupting
- being absent without stated reason and without leaving a contact number
- destroying other people's orders of priorities by continually demanding pieces of work
- being insensitive to other people's unspoken feelings and ideas
- dropping in 'for a couple of minutes' and wasting the whole afternoon
- forgetting to mention important items — especially informal decisions made over lunch or in the corridor.

People may not like us popping up unexpectedly, but they moan if they never see us. The rule when we walk the job (see Chapter 1) is to have a reason for being there: it is awkward to be cast in the role of visiting VIP and embarrassing to be mistaken for the electrician. Equally, a 'private eye' approach will merely generate 'alibis'. Show genuine interest, listen, and take notes and put down what the other person wants you to remember — you can always make your own notes afterwards. Let the person have your reactions or answers within 48 hours — even (or perhaps especially) when the answer is no.

Listening has been called the 'lost art of our age'. We have already seen how much faster we can think than the other person can talk. Use your eyes and ears to search for what they mean rather than what they actually say. Try not to let your mind wander, no matter what the distraction.

When you are trying to uncover facts at selection, appraisal, grievance or disciplinary meetings, the art of listening becomes especially important. You can fail by:

- forgetting to remain neutral
- misunderstanding
- jumping to conclusions
- dealing prematurely with situations
- rejecting the other person's explanation without really thinking about it.

Failures of this type can lead to serious consequences. The subordinate concerned is likely to lapse into hostility, suspicious withdrawal or passive acceptance, and the end result is a sullen team, slavishly performing their tasks, convinced that it doesn't pay to think for themselves.

A team leader in one of The Industrial Society's action-centred leadership courses was once listening as other delegates discussed how she had coped with leading four others in an exercise. 'But we were given only twenty minutes!' she protested. True — if just the elapsed time was counted. But in fact the team was five-strong, so she had a total of 100 'people-minutes' to play with. As soon as she realised this, her managerial skills took a great leap forward.

People need managers who are expert and friendly, managers who respect their time and aspirations, leaders who can extract the utmost from all those precious 'people-minutes'.

Your secretary

Look at one secretary, sitting there mute and resentful. She's all right for typing and filing, but she made a mess of her last little task through nervousness, and so it was no wonder Herbert took it over and finished it off himself. He still drafts all his correspondence in longhand and opens all his own mail. She's just itching for 5.30.

Up on the 11th floor Harriet is talking about her secretary. 'Ideal. Does everything for me. Finds things I used to lose. Wasn't she tactful about you turning up like this? Anyway, we'd better be brisk: she'll be here in a minute to drag me off to that meeting.'

What a contrast between the two different secretaries . . . only, they're not two different secretaries. They're the same one, six months apart.

Secretaries can tackle many of their boss's tasks on their own. This releases the boss's time for something else, and saves money because, justly or unjustly, the boss earns more than the secretary. This increased efficiency is not achieved by magic, although some say 'chemistry' comes into it.

Harriet holds fortnightly 'business meetings' with her secretary. They discuss their work as partners in a joint enterprise.

Many managers still expect a brand-new secretary to plunge straight in — 'type all right, can you?' is the full extent of the briefing for the job. But time spent at the start of the partnership can save costly mistakes and vast amounts of time later.

Many secretaries complain of silent, disappearing bosses who hardly ever speak except to deliver dictation and who vanish without saying where they are going. Conflict can arise from the differing expectations of the boss and the secretary. This difficulty can be overcome by regular 'business meetings' as well as by the use of target setting (*see* Chapter 4). Managers should be sure that the targets they set their secretaries should not all be boring ones: the more secretaries are required to use their initiative, the better.

A suitable agenda for the 'business meeting' might contain the following items:

- results of any meeting you have attended without your secretary
- future plans affecting the department's workload
- reallocation of priorities so that the secretary's time can be appropriately organised
- checking of diaries to ensure that the same appointments appear in both
- review of telephone calls, action taken, and advice for action needed
- potential office problems you might not have heard about.

If you've a good partnership, you'll recognise that your secretary is a person rather than just a tool. He or she will attend at least some meetings with you; will occasionally represent you or even the organisation; will give their own name on the telephone and will append his or her own name (rather than just 'pp' over your name) to letters; will know the department's budget, income and expenditure; will have full responsibility for at least one project, not necessarily 'secretarial'; will have a job description with performance standards linked to your own — in short, will be rather like an extra 'you'.

More time

Most of us, given the time, would do more of what we are paid to do.

We have seen what takes up so much time, seducing us away from what we should be doing. High on the list are the brief contacts and queries and the mundane day-to-day tasks. We get trapped into attempting to control failures when we should be monitoring progress. It would be nice to do the coping at the start, instead of trying to cobble everything together at the last moment.

Planning is not so much an art as a craft, and we can set out simple guidelines. Some of these things we do instinctively, others need to be thought about:

- set long-term objectives
- gather facts (opinions, feelings) relevant to the long term (which can be anything from one week to five years)
- sort out the facts under various appropriate headings
- figure out the relationships and priorities between the various elements
- draw up more than one long-term plan
- try to forecast (that is, guess) the probable outcome of each plan
- select the plan that most closely fits the long-term objective
- set each short-term objective in turn
- gather facts (opinions, feelings) relevant to the short term (which can be anything from a few hours to a year).

Now, what can we plan? There are some things we can't: changes in legislation, breakdowns, delivery failures, industrial troubles in other organisations, and so on. These just have to be coped with when they happen. But we can plan the mundane elements — the routine. We need to rid ourselves of the notion that the word 'routine' means just 'boring'. Routines were invented in the first place to ensure the success of the total enterprise. For all the statements of objectives, the job descriptions and the checklists, the rule books and the manuals of procedure, it is what we do that turns the dream into reality. Routines help us, step by step, to reach our goal. They are recurrent, and therefore predictable — and so they can be planned.

When every member of the team is doing their bit, the efforts of all the team members combine to take us on our way. It is our common purpose that lends dignity to the process. We'll know we're getting somewhere when the manager is purely 'accountable' — that is, when all the others in the team are 'responsible'. It is then our privilege to generate the activities of the rest, and to support them in what they are doing.

Before we leave the subject of time, here are a few final tips (in no particular order):

- study recurrent crises and find out ways of planning ahead to avoid them

- spend more time in future on upward rather than downward communication
- think about the boss's problems
- keep all your scribbled notes, telephone-message slips, doodles and so on for a period of one month; if you analyse them you may find clues about how to save time next month
- draw up an occasional 'laundry list' of detailed activities during a period of 30 minutes, and see where the time went
- not how long things actually take
- develop a daily/weekly/monthly/annual 'timetable', and encourage others to do the same
- learn when to say no
- from time to time, think about what you'll do when you retire
- get well acquainted with modern mathematical and statistical methods
- find out the basics of the new technology (computers, word processors, etc.): even if it all seems irrelevant to your job now, you may very well find that tomorrow your knowledge of hi-tech will save countless hours
- ask other people what devices they use to save time.

8 SELECTION

Many managers make no secret of the fact that they dislike interviewing job candidates. Others believe that they are good at interviewing, and therefore enjoy it. However, very few of us interview on a systematic and logical basis, and with planned follow-up. The result is that, all too often, staff are taken on after only the most subjective and inaccurate examination of their ability and suitability to do the job. Failure to make the right choice is costly in terms of staff turnover and can jeopardise the efficiency of the whole organisation. Moreover, it doesn't do the wrongly appointed candidate any favours either, because the psychological trauma of being found apparently incompetent can do great damage to that person's confidence — especially if they are, in fact, perfectly able and competent, but are just not right for this job.

Selecting people for jobs

In our context, the word 'selection' means choosing the person who will give our organisation the results that it wants from a particular job. It follows that any selection that does not give the organisation the required results is wasting money.

Inadequacies, of course, cannot be measured simply in terms of job performance. An employee might be extremely capable at their job but be destructive, unfriendly or uncooperative towards colleagues. This will upset the harmony that needs to exist if people are to give of their best — and that, again, will lose the organisation money.

For all of these reasons, you must look very closely at a person's skills and characteristics before taking the very major step of choosing that person to do a job for your organisation.

Who selects?

Most companies have a personnel officer or department, one of whose duties is the selection of people for jobs. Sadly, this responsibility has often been allowed to pass completely from the line manager to the personnel specialist. At best, you may sit in quietly for part of the interview. At worst, the first you know of a new recruit is when the person turns up for work the first morning, with the result that the recruit may prove unable to do the job to your satisfaction or may simply not fit in with the team. Such situations could be largely avoided if line managers were actively involved in the selection process.

If you are to be held accountable for a new employee's future performance, you must have a say in choosing the employee. Of course, the special skills of the personnel department should be used to attract recruits, filter out the non-starters, and pick out those of a candidate's positive characteristics that a non-specialist might miss, but before the final decision is made you should have the right to recommend the acceptance or rejection of a candidate. Anything less is unfair to you, your organisation and the potential employee.

Obviously the line manager knows more about what the job entails than do the personnel specialists, but there is an equally important reason why you should be the person responsible for the candidate being taken on. The single aspect of a job that can do most to inspire, motivate and commit an employee is that person's attitude to the boss or leader. This boss/subordinate relationship should be developed as soon as possible. What better way to start than for new employees to know that they were chosen for the job by the person for whom they are going to work, rather than by 'some bod in the personnel department'?

A vacancy arises

People resign for all sorts of reasons. Sometimes that reason is unavoidable — pregnancy, age, illness. Often, too, the reasons are understandable and the organisation has little choice but to accept them — a higher salary elsewhere, for instance. At times, however, the reasons are such that they point to a failure somewhere within the organisation. Examples are dissatisfaction (with job, prospects or conditions), conflict (with colleagues or boss), and resentment concerning perceived injustice within the organisation.

If someone is leaving for one of these latter reasons the organisation has a problem which should be looked into immediately. For, if one person is affected this way, others will be, too, and dissatisfied or disgruntled employees are expensive — whether they leave the company or not.

What can you do? The answer is to conduct a termination interview to find out as quickly and accurately as possible why a person is leaving.

The timing of the interview is important. If it is held as soon as the resignation has been received, you may be able to persuade the employee to stay — if that is what you want. Otherwise, it is better to wait until the final day, when the person is more likely to tell you what is really wrong.

Some leavers prefer to deal with someone who they feel is neutral, so termination interviews are often carried out by the personnel officer. If so, you must be sure to find out from the personnel officer afterwards what points were made. Where possible, however, it makes sense for you to conduct the interview. For the interview to be of any value, leavers must be made to feel free to say whatever they think without contradiction or defence, and it must be guaranteed that everything said about other employees will be in strict confidence.

It is important that all the other employees should see that the faults brought to light at the interview are corrected as swiftly as possible. However, be warned: if the interview is as frank as it should be, you may hear a thing or two you'll wish you hadn't!

Sometimes you'll discover from the interview that the trouble is that some flaw in the organisation or department has meant that the leaver's job has been either too difficult or too easy, too busy or not busy enough. If so, you must think carefully about the nature of the job before seeking to recruit someone new. Far too often, the immediate move taken after someone has resigned is to try to find the same type of person as held the job before. Perhaps you really need a different type of person, or maybe two people are required to do the job, or maybe the duties of the various people within the department should be shuffled around a little.

Alternatively, should the job be filled at all? Very often jobs exist for no better reason than that they have always existed in the past. The newly vacated job should be looked at critically to see what its purpose really is: if it doesn't have one, you should get rid of it.

Even if it does have a purpose, the vacancy still provides a golden opportunity to restructure a department or area more efficiently; or to give someone a short burst of experience in that job; or to make the jobs of the other people in the department more enjoyable by splitting up the duties among them, giving them more responsibility and more control over their own jobs.

Before you can come to a final decision as to whether or how a vacancy needs to be filled, you should draw up a job description, along the lines discussed on pages 39-41. Really, you need two descriptions: one drawn up by you and the other drawn up by the person who's leaving, assuming they haven't already left (in which case you'll have to make do with the notes from the termination interview). The two descriptions will almost certainly be different — as we saw in the preceding chapter — with the truth lying somewhere between the two. Once you know what the job actually is you can think sensibly about what sort of recruit, if any, you are looking for.

If, incidentally, the two descriptions are totally different, the situation is worth close attention. There are probably several areas of responsibility which nobody is looking after for the simple reason that you think the subordinate is doing them and the subordinate thinks you are.

Who should fill the vacancy?

Just as, in engineering, a specification is produced to prescribe the sort of machine that is needed to do a job satisfactorily, in selection a specification is produced to prescribe the sort of person required.

By far the most widely accepted and useful method for producing such a specification — although by no means the only or necessarily the best one — is the 'Seven Point Plan' produced by Alex Rodger at The National Institute of Industrial Psychology. Of its seven headings we shall cover here only the five that are most easily and reasonably usable by the line manager. Where personnel specialists exist in companies, managers can safely leave the finer details of the 'Seven Point Plan' to them. Where there is no such specialist, it may be advisable for you to receive some training in this field from one of the recognised authorities.

The method involved in the Plan is to look at the job description under several major headings. Under each heading you specify what is wanted in the candidate, thereby producing a 'personnel specification'. It is useful to state whether the aspects required are 'essential' (the candidate must have them to be able to do the job satisfactorily) or 'desirable' (the candidate who possesses these will probably do the job particularly well). Ideally, the candidate will have the full gamut of both essential and desirable aspects but, not only are such paragons rare, it may be a mistake to employ too many of them: a department full of 'stars' will soon generate problems in terms of job satisfaction, motivation and career progress.

The five specific headings we shall look at are:

- physical requirements
- attainments
- abilities
- disposition
- circumstances.

Physical requirements

These are the aspects of health, physique, appearance, bearing and so on that may be important to the job. For example, you would not wish to give a heavy labouring job to someone with a history of back complaints, while for a 'stressful' job you would be seeking someone with a calm, relaxed manner and an even temperament. However, that said, there is no point in putting restrictions on the type of candidate sought unless you have to and unless they are derived from the actual requirements of the job.

An obvious area where this applies is in the field of the disabled. A company in South Wales has a receptionist who is one of the most efficient, helpful and courteous in his job that you could imagine. He is in fact blind. Most clerical and many process-line jobs today do not require the employee to move around much, if at all, and so there is absolutely no reason why these and many other jobs should not be done by disabled people — thereby providing an extra source of potentially excellent recruits for your organisation.

Attainments

There are three major areas here. First is education: must the job holder have a certain educational qualification in some particular subject? For example, an accounts clerk will probably need to have some sort of paper qualification in mathematics, and a secretary likewise in English language. Then there is work qualification: the job may well require an apprenticeship, or a particular City and Guilds endorsement, or typing and shorthand certificates to a certain level. Finally, there is job experience: what sort of a job history should potential employees have had if they are to do a job satisfactorily?

Abilities

Different abilities are required for different jobs. Some can really be measured only by tests which have to be applied by someone trained in their use. However, there are many abilities which line managers can test themselves — for example, giving an electrician a wiring diagram and asking questions about it, or asking a mechanic to diagnose a fault. The classic example is, of course, giving a would-be secretary a shorthand and typing test.

Disposition

It is important to decide what sort of personality someone should have if he or she is to do the job properly. For example, an independent or creative person is unlikely to settle down happily on the assembly line, and an indecisive person is probably not the best appointee for the post of quality-control inspector.

What you are really asking is: what sort of candidate would fit, as a person, into the particular job in question (and, indeed, into the organisation)? This is really very important because, as we have already said, even the most highly skilled and able employees are no use at all if they can't fit in.

Circumstances

If a job involves awkward hours, peculiar shifts or a lot of travel — in other words, anything unusual — it is important to check that this will be allowed by the candidate's domestic circumstances. If the person lives with an aged relative who cannot be left alone for long periods then this obviously inhibits travel, for example.

It helps to know how committed candidates are to their district. Do they come from the area? Are they buying a house? Are their children at school nearby? All can be useful pointers as to whether they will stay with you long or, looked at the other way, if they will be prepared to move should the organisation do so. And, of course, it is useful to know how far potential employees will have to travel to work each day. 'A lift with a friend' over 15 miles is sure to generate problems at some time or another!

It must be emphasised that the requirements given under the five headings above are guidelines to help in selection: they don't provide a blueprint for choosing the perfect employee. At best they represent an attempt to apply some logic to a highly problematical activity.

Here is the personnel specification used by a course administrator of The Industrial Society to appoint his secretary:

Description:		This job is one which is divided equally between secretarial duties for a management and training adviser and the administration of courses in a particular field
Physical:	Essential:	Good health record
		Clear, pleasant telephone voice
	Desirable:	Over 20, under 30
Attainments:	Essential:	O-level (or equivalent) English language
		Typing — 40wpm
	Desirable:	A-level English
		Shorthand or Speedwriting — 80wpm
		Previous experience of training department; course administration
Abilities:	Essential:	Good layout of typing
		Above-average spelling
Disposition:	Essential:	Able to work without direction
		Able to work with others
		Flexible

		Desirable:	Sense of humour
			Lively
Circumstances:		Essential:	Reasonable and reliable travel to office
		Desirable:	Living locally
			Telephone at home
			Willing to be away from home occasionally

Where will we find the right person?

The first place you should look in your search for recruits is within your own organisation. Most companies today notify all vacancies to their employees, and some also use vacancies as training experiences for up-and-coming personnel. A few have an effective management-development system linked to a realistic appraisal system (*see* Chapter 3) which can produce the replacements virtually automatically. You can be fairly sure that, whatever method (if any) operates, there are people within your organisation who ought at least to be considered. Failure to make use of these people is a major waste of resources and a sure way of 'demotivating' staff. Come to that, it is a sure way of losing them: if they cannot obtain promotion in your organisation they are sure to go to one where they can.

Sometimes, of course, the internal candidates are not good enough or, for some reason, it makes good sense to look outside. Advertising is always expensive, and can often be ineffectual. For example, one company spent years advertising in the local press for operators and never had a very good response. One day they put up a notice outside the factory gate and had an immediate response, because potential recruits saw the sign as they travelled to and from work. The cost? Next to nothing.

Where press advertising is necessary, you or your personnel specialist would do well to get hold of an expert. Remember, advertising is expensive: you want to make sure you get the maximum results for every pound you spend. Most reputable advertising agencies obtain their commission from the newspapers and journals that carry the advertisement, not from the company that places it. So, for no fee to you, you get professional advice on where to place the advertisement and how to word it.

If you decide to draw up your own advertisement, however, try to emphasise that aspect of the position which will most appeal to potential candidates. This is not necessarily the salary (many advertisements make no mention of salary): it can often be status, conditions, security, or the challenge of a particular job.

If the advertisement is well designed and based upon the personnel specification you have drawn up, it should not produce hundreds of replies. Ideally, it should produce several candidates, all of whom are real contenders for the job, and at least one of whom will be as near ideal as possible.

Another method of external recruitment is through government agencies. Invariably it pays dividends to talk over your recruitment needs with them, preferably inviting them to come to the organisation to see and discuss at first hand the problems and probable solutions. Commercial agencies (usually called 'bureaux') have their uses, particularly for secretarial or junior staff; and for more senior staff you may choose to use a recruitment agency.

How do we choose which person?

Application forms are usually a good thing. The form itself should be pleasant to look at, with clear questions and enough space to allow the candidate to answer them fully.

Once the form has been completed and returned, the next step is to compare it with the personnel specification. If it fails to meet any of the essential requirements, the applicant must be rejected for this particular post — although it may be worth considering them for another within the organisation.

In some cases no candidate may meet all the essential requirements. This may mean that the original personnel specification was overambitious, or that the type of candidate required is not available. Either way, you must decide whether to readvertise, hoping for better luck next time, or just take the best of those available.

Application forms are not a good idea when you are seeking, for example, unskilled shop-floor personnel. Good candidates for such positions may not find it easy first to telephone and then to fill in the form. Since literacy and use of the telephone are not part of their job requirements, why make them so? For this is what you are in effect doing. You would do much better to encourage such potential employees to come to the company, where they can be interviewed by someone who can fill in the form as they go along. Of course, this takes longer, but if it attracts the applicants you want then it is worth it.

One vital aspect of recruitment is the public image of the organisation. If it is good, applicants will be attracted; if it isn't, they won't. Part of this image is based on the way the organisation treats job applicants. Make sure that all applications are acknowledged immediately, and let candidates know as soon as possible if you are taking things further or not. If not, the letter should be sympathetic and should thank the candidate for their interest. If you plan to consider the candidate further, the letter should explain what will happen next.

The interview

When a candidate comes for interview, make sure everyone concerned knows the person's name — the security guard at the gate, the receptionist, the secretary, and so on. Candidates are bound to be pleased to find that they are expected. Make sure there is somewhere quiet and comfortable where the candidate can relax while waiting for the interview. There should be reading material and access to lavatories.

If a true picture is to be obtained, the candidate must feel relaxed during the interview itself. Choose a comfortable, private room where there will be as few distractions as possible: have telephone calls transferred elsewhere, and make sure you put them at their ease. Often it is better to use two fairly comfortable chairs with a low table next to them on which to rest coffee cups, papers and so on. Conversely, some people find this informality off-putting, and actually prefer it if the interviewer is safely tucked away behind a desk. Judge each situation on its own merits.

Before the interview you should have looked over the candidate's application form to familiarise yourself with the candidate's history and, by comparing it with the personnel specification, to pick out the points that need to be investigated further. Using both documents, you should then prepare a plan of how you want the interview to go, in terms of areas to be explored. Of course, the interview itself will have to be very flexible, depending on the candidate, but a plan helps the interview to be systematic and ensures nothing important is left out.

It is probably a good idea to think about what sort of question you will start with. The candidate will probably still be tense at the beginning, so a neutral question is usually best. A good topic might be how the person travelled to the interview: 'Did you have a good journey?' This does not put the candidate under any pressure, but does elicit some useful information — how far they will have to commute if they are offered the job, and whether their travel arrangements, assuming they get the job, are likely to cause problems.

It is important that you should be clear about your objectives for the interview. They are:

- to find out whether or not the candidate is suitable for the job and the organisation
- to find out, conversely, whether the job and the organisation are suitable for the candidate
- to make the candidate feel that, even if ultimately rejected, they had a fair deal (this is part of the public-image concern we mentioned earlier).

The importance of the first two cannot be overemphasised. Nonetheless, while few people would forget about the first, the second is often overlooked. Yet the commitment of employees to an organisation that suits them is crucial to its profitability and effectiveness.

At the start of the interview you should check the interviewee's name — people have been known to interview the wrong person! Introduce yourself, and settle down with the candidate. It is best to supply an ashtray, even if you don't smoke yourself: you want the candidate to relax, after all. You should then use your prepared opening question to break the ice, and tell the candidate that this is really a two-way discussion. It is amazing how often interviewees are surprised to be told that they are expected to gain as well as give information at the interview. It is a good idea to stress that, if unsure about something, the candidate should feel free to ask questions — you too can learn from their questions.

You should ask if the interviewee objects to your taking notes 'purely as reminders of the more important facts that come up'. This slightly flattering approach invariably produces assent. The notes themselves should be no more than short phrases or trigger-words, just enough to remind you to return to a point later or to summarise at the end. A useful tip is not to make a note immediately after an interviewee has said something against themselves but to wait until the conversation has moved on to something else.

After the ice has been broken it is a good idea to go on by giving some information about the vacancy. Run briefly through a general description of the job, the department, the company, the people involved, the prospects, and the job's terms and conditions. If there are a lot of people to be interviewed, or if you are pressed for time, it is a good idea to produce a broad outline of these facts on paper and give a copy to each candidate to read immediately before their interview; however, still make sure the candidate is given the opportunity to ask questions in this area.

It is worth saving a fully detailed description of the job and so on until after the main interview because:

- you can waste a great deal of time telling candidates about the job only to discover during the interview that they are totally unsuited for it
- clever candidates can use the details given at the outset to give the answers they know the interviewer is seeking, rather than the 'real' ones.

During the interview proper, you should use your prepared plan and the personnel specification to make sure you work through all the relevant areas, collecting facts and the candidate's opinions as you go along. Make sure you really do get all the facts you need — after the interview is too late. Also, you should probe beyond the surface of the facts presented to you. For example, if the candidate is a supervisor in her current job you should ask how many people she supervises, how many jobs they tackle, and what her actual responsibilities are. If you do not, then the datum you have recorded is largely meaningless.

If you are to get a realistic picture of the candidate you must get the candidate to talk. A sure way of not doing so is to ask questions that require only a 'yes' or 'no' answer. Instead, ask open-ended questions that force the candidate to broaden the scope of the replies. For example, the question 'Did you enjoy your last job?' elicits a 'yes' or a 'no', but 'What did you think of your last job?' requires the candidate to express an opinion.

Open-ended questions will lead on to other — probably more specific — questions.

Often the interviewee will, for a number of reasons, leave out facts or bend them slightly so that they show in a favourable light. If you are listening and observing carefully, you should be able to spot when this is happening and explore the relevant issues in more depth. Nervousness on particular questions may possibly be a sign of extra tension caused by telling a half-truth or even a lie.

Another advantage of concentrating like this is that it impresses on the candidate their importance both to you and to the organisation. The candidate is therefore much more likely really to open up — with obvious benefits to you.

We have used the word 'objectivity' several times, and it is worth remembering that, just as no candidate can be completely objective about themselves, neither can you, as interviewer, be totally objective about the person unless you make a really big effort to recognise and accept this failing, and compensate for it. You should watch out particularly for positive and negative bias towards the interviewee. An example of positive bias might be that you assumed the candidate was 'one of the good guys' because he or she came from the same town as you, played the same sport, or was incredibly good-looking. Negative bias might come about because you disliked a person's hairstyle or accent. Either form of bias is a danger: your job is to obtain the facts about a person and compare them objectively with the requirements in the specification.

Only after you have done this should your subjective judgement come into play, and even then it should be an honest one, uninfluenced by your own private likes and dislikes, Interviewers who say they can judge candidates 'just by looking at them' are doing themselves, the candidate and the organisation a great disservice.

One small — but sometimes not so small — point concerns union membership. You should familiarise yourself with any arrangements that exist between the company and any trade unions. You should give the candidate the relevant facts, and make sure no problems are likely to arise.

Once you have got all you need from the candidate you should, after checking the interviewee has no further questions, make it clear that the interview is over. You should check that the candidate's travelling expenses have been covered, tell the candidate what will be the next stage of the process and when it will happen, thank them for coming, and finally see them to the door.

The decision

After all the candidates have been interviewed you have the tricky task of analysing the results. Some candidates will have fallen by the wayside because of obvious unsuitability, but you will almost certainly find that there are still several who are worth considering. A good way of getting some kind of objective measure of their worth is to work through the personnel specification assessing each candidate against each requirement using a scale something like this:

A = much above average = 150%
B = above average = 125%
C = average = 100%
D = below average = 75%
E = much below average = 50%

The ideal candidate, bearing in mind that the specification describes a person who will do the job satisfactorily, will have all Cs. Anyone with As or Es is probably too good or too bad for the job. Someone with lots of Bs is probably acceptable, so long as there is likely to be room for them to move upwards in a year or so. Someone with lots of Ds may suffice, but will need training.

Very often one factor (for example, attainments) will be of particular importance — you should decide if this is the case when drawing up the specification. The effect of this special importance is to weight your decision; for example, if attainments are important and the candidate has a C in this area, one other C plus three Ds should be enough to raise the overall rating to C.

Some companies use a standard interview assessment form which requires you to put down your comments, assessments and decisions under various headings. The value of such a system is that it enables one candidate to be compared with another fairly objectively. This is particularly useful if one person is seen at 10.00am on Monday and the next on Friday at 5.00pm.

Another useful guide is to imagine each candidate in typical situations involved with the job and consider how they might get on.

Once you've weighed all the facts, there still remains the vital matter of personality. If you and the candidate dislike each other on sight there really isn't too much point in going on, even if the candidate fits the qualifications perfectly. However, it might be that the candidate could work perfectly well with someone else, so it is worth recommending the person to several managers to see if one of them can make use of the person's skills.

You should make a record of the bare bones of the interview, noting especially the reasons why rejected candidates have been rejected. Should one of them allege discrimination through race, sex, union membership, criminal record, sexual predilection or whatever it is up to the company concerned to prove its innocence. In such a situation, records of the decision and the reasons for it can be invaluable.

If you decide you would like to offer the job to a candidate, you still have some work to do first. The major chore concerns references.

Written testimonials brought to the interview should be treated warily unless you can verify them with the company concerned. Even so, the normal type of written reference is not a lot of use: it tells you what a jolly worth person the candidate is, and very little else. You can do much better by writing to the referee asking such specific questions as:

- What are the dates between which the candidate worked for you?
- What was the job title?
- What did the job involve
- What was the rate of pay?
- How many days' sickness did the person have in the last two years?

and, the clincher:

- Would you re-employ this person?

You may find the company will refuse to answer some or all of these questions. If they do respond, do not pay too much attention to favourable references, because people like to be charitable in such matters. If they give a bad reference, on the other hand, you should look into the matter more deeply — bearing in mind, however, that it may well be that the candidate's version of events is the true one.

Placement and follow-up

Assuming the candidate has accepted your offer and that the medical tests (if any) and references are all right, you should take steps to ensure that the new employee will be received properly on the first day, and will be given any training necessary to make them an effective member of the organisation as soon as possible.

Once the employee has been fully inducted and has settled in, you should stand back and, over the next few months, keep a careful eye on them to make sure they really are the person you thought they would be at the interview. If not, what did you miss or wrongly interpret, and what can you do to avoid making the same mistake next time?

For the short term, clues will turn up at appraisal interviews (*see* Chapter 3). And, if it comes to it, the termination interview will also give very good feedback on the validity of the choice and the system which brought you to make it.

9 TRAINING

Your role in training is vitally important. You are uniquely placed to decide who needs to be trained, and to determine the training needs of those whom you manage. You are also the only person in a position to measure the return on training investment — by monitoring the progress of employees before and after training. Training specialists can provide help and advice, but they can be effective only if they have active cooperation from you.

Why train?

Training is the planned provision of the means of learning either on the job or in a training centre. It helps employees to do their present or future jobs competently, thereby increasing both the organisation's efficiency and their own job satisfaction. The benefits of training can be summarised as follows:

- reduction of the time and cost of learning, because people do the job quickly, safely, to the standards required, and with minimum waste of materials or damage to equipment
- improved job performance, in terms of increased output, improved quality, and ability to get the job done on time
- less supervision required, because problems such as absenteeism, lateness and accidents decline owing to the greater motivation (*see* Chapter 2) that training brings
- more satisfactory recruitment and selection, because the prospect of training attracts the right type of job applicants
- reduced labour turnover, because people are gaining more job satisfaction and enjoying the fact that their potential is being developed.

All of these benefits together bring two further ones: reduced running costs to the organisation and, through improvement in the quality of goods and services, greater customer satisfaction.

Training is the responsibility of managers, all the way down from the top executive to the front-line supervisor because, if we are to make sure the job is done successfully, we must ensure that effectiveness of the employees doing the actual work is maintained at as high a level as possible.

Who is to be trained?

Various types of employees require training, the most obvious category being new entrants. Before looking at them, however, let's glance swiftly at the other categories.

Some employees need training to become better at their present job. Regular appraisal (*see* Chapter 3) will show you which employees these are, and in which areas the training is required. Other employees require training with a view to promotion, and individual employees require opportunities to develop their latent talents and abilities. Change (*see* Chapter 10) — whether in the social climate, legislation, technology, or whatever — frequently requires that employees be retrained to gain new knowledge and skills to cope either with jobs that are essentially new or that, although they are still the same jobs, are now being done in different ways.

Employees nearing retirement are in a training category of their own. It is in both their own interests and those of the organisation that such employees, while maintaining adequate performance and making full use of the knowledge and experience they have, should be able to 'run down' in preparation for their retirement. Some may learn new skills — becoming job instructors, for example — or be asked to apply their experience to special projects which do not fit easily into the normal routine. Others may have to be trained to accept lower-level jobs for the last few years of their working lives.

However, as noted, new entrants are probably the major category of trainees. School-leavers and graduates are unlikely to have any knowledge or experience either of the type of work they are to do or of the conditions under which it is to be carried out. Other people joining the company may have previous work experience, but it will not necessarily be relevant.

All new employees therefore require induction training in order to familiarise themselves with the organisation, its products and/or services, its personnel policies and its practices. Part of this training may be carried out by the personnel department, but it is your responsibility to introduce newcomers to your own department, to train them from the start in the way it is run, and to imprint in them the standards of performance and behaviour expected from them.

The importance of induction can't be overemphasised, especially where young employees are concerned: the attitudes to work they acquire now will probably last the rest of their lives. If you fail to give the necessary time and attention to this aspect of training you will probably find a lot of new employees leaving again within their first few months, and, among those who stay, poor timekeeping, absenteeism, and a general lack of interest in the work and commitment to the organisation.

The sort of information you should give to new employees is listed below. Note, however, that you should not give all this information to new employees at once — it is too much to digest. Give them the essential information about their own job and the department first. However, here is the full list:

Information about organisation:
- name
- history
- organisation chart
- products and/or services
- customers
- location(s).

Information about department:
- what it makes or what services it gives
- where it fits into the organisation
- jobs done (including the trainee's, and where it fits in)
- departmental rules (timekeeping, meal breaks, safety, smoking, etc.)
- supervision (including names)
- other employees (including names)
- work relationships.

Employment conditions:
- pay
- make-up of pay (bonus or other plus rates, overtime, deductions)

- method of payment (how, where, when)
- hours of work (normal, overtime, weekends, shifts)
- holidays
- sickness payment scheme
- pension scheme
- bonuses or profit-sharing
- notice period
- time-recording and timekeeping
- absence (notification, certificates, pay).

Health, safety, welfare:
- medical examination(s)
- medical/first-aid facilities
- toilet and cloakroom facilities
- hygiene (personal/process)
- safety (regulations, appliances)
- protective clothing
- fire-precaution procedures
- canteen facilities
- sports and/or social club
- savings schemes
- purchase facilities
- parking
- travelling arrangements
- telephone calls
- time off
- loans
- personal problems.

General:
- joint consultation (works/staff advisory committee)
- grievance/disciplinary procedures
- trade-union membership
- education and training
- promotions and transfers
- suggestions scheme
- security arrangements.

New employees seldom bring to the job the full range of knowledge and skills required, so as well as receiving induction training they must be trained in the necessary job knowledge and skills. You should know which gaps require filling in these areas because of the comparison you made, during the selection period (see Chapter 8), between the personnel specification and the particular candidate's qualities.

What training is to be done?

For training to be effective you must first decide in some detail what specific knowledge and skills the job involves, what the individual already possesses, and what gaps training can realistically fill. To do this most effectively you need to take a systematic approach to identifying training requirements. Also, you may need to enlist the help of a training specialist of some kind.

First you should make a preliminary examination of the job to find out what is required to ensure it is done satisfactorily. You may think you already know all the jobs in your department — in which case you could be in for a shock, as we noted in chapter 4. Observe the whole job, and question the job-holder about the nature of the activities involved in it. This is especially important when it comes to training new employees to take over an existing job, because the previous job-holder may have modified it quite a lot to suit their own strengths and weaknesses. Such variations may suit neither the new employee nor you.

Next, prepare a job description (see Chapter 3), preferably in conjunction with an employee doing the same job. If the existing job-holder is leaving and the new entrant is taking over, either get the current incumbent to produce their version of the job description (to compare with your own) or carry out an effective termination interview, as detailed in Chapter 8.

Third, analyse the training requirements. Examine the main activities given in the job description to identify the tasks involved and the knowledge and skills required. The extent and depth of this examination obviously depend on the complexity of the job concerned. Here it is best to ask for the help of a specialist, such as your organisation's training officer. The result of the analysis will be a job specification, a summary of the specific knowledge and skills required but not necessarily in the order in which they should be taught.

Finally, assess the performance of the individual. The new employee's degree of competence to perform the job should have been assessed during selection. Existing job-holders need regular appraisal to determine (a) how they are measuring up to required performance standards, and (b) what training they need either to make good their deficiencies or to develop their potential. This assessment will render a detailed statement of what they need to learn; that is, a training specification. In the case of the new employee, of course, the job specification and the training specification are essentially the same thing.

Identification of training requirements is not related solely to the individual. You need to be alert to the training implications, both for your own department and for the organisation as a whole, of such matters as technological developments, new systems and procedures, market forecasts, changes in employment policies and practices. Such changes may call for a one-off programme to meet a temporary situation or an emergency. However, if the organisation is to achieve its objectives there must be a continuous review of manpower resources to ensure their effective use throughout the organisation.

The training programme

You are, clearly, responsible for the training of your staff; but in many respects you are also the best person actually to do the training. You know the jobs (or should!), you know your staff, and you have a direct interest in a successful outcome.

The way training is carried out will depend on various factors — such as the numbers to be trained and the facilities at your disposal. Training can be done (a) on the job, (b) off the job but within the organisation, or (c) off the job and outside the organisation.

A training programme will employ one or more of these means, depending on what is best in the circumstances and most suited to the particular situation. The programme should contain all the items in the training specification and give details of the order in which they should be taught, the methods to be used, instructional staff, location(s) and a timetable. In planning the programme, you should ask yourself:

- who is to be trained?   (number and type of employees)
- why are they to be trained?   (training objectives)
- what should they be taught?   (knowledge and skills)
- how should training be done?   (methods)

- who should do the training? (instructors)
- when can it be done? (length and frequency of sessions)
- where will it be done? (location)
- how will it be assessed? (evaluation).

When you are designing the programme you should consider the following points:

- sequence: chronological, in order of priority, or taking common/related items together?
- load and pace: how much information can trainees absorb, and how quickly?
- variety: what subject matter, what methods?
- feedback: how will you test learning — by target setting (*see* Chapter 4), exercises, or what?

Keeping simple records can help you decide who needs training and when, and ensure that all staff are receiving the required training. You should have an individual record for each trainee, giving name, department, date of joining, and details of the training; and a department record, giving names of trainees, type of training, dates, results of training, costs, and further action taken.

Methods of training

Here we'll look briefly at the main training methods, how they're used, and some of their advantages (labelled good) and drawbacks (bad).

Assignments/projects

For individual or group training. This form of exercise requires trainees to complete a definite task, usually with a time limit. These tasks should be based on actual problems facing the trainees' department or organisation. The exercises are used to give trainees practical experience in applying the knowledge and skills they've learned through formal education or previous training.

Trainees should be given briefs written in clear, specific terms; for example, 'List the causes of all time-losing accidents in the machine shop during the last two years, and suggest how they could be prevented in future.' The brief should also include reference to the type and sources of information required.

The amount of guidance you give will depend on the trainees' level of competence and the complexity of the problem but, in general, the more the trainees are left to themselves the better. They should produce specific, practical answers which take account of the policies, practices and general constraints of the situation. The results of their efforts should be assessed by you as well as by anyone else relevant to the problem.

Good: training activities are directly related to the practicalities of the job; this method provides a simple means of monitoring progress and evaluating the effectiveness of the training itself; recommendations from the trainees may be adopted, and the 'pay off' measured in financial terms.

Bad: this method can make great demands on the time of a number of senior people.

Business exercises (in-tray)

For group training; adaptable for individuals. In-tray exercises simulate real life by presenting trainees with a number of items — letters, memos, reports, and so on — similar to those which arrive on their own desks. They must deal with these by writing down whatever actions they think appropriate in the circumstances described in the exercise. The results of their efforts are analysed and discussed.

Good: like all business games and exercises, this can provide realistic experience of the techniques and skills required in the job.

Bad: the benefit is realised only if the exercise material selected is relevant to the needs of the trainees.

Business games

For group training. In these exercises groups of trainees representing imaginary organisations (or parts thereof) operate in a defined situation.

A wide variety of business games exists. A common type involves planning a plant, staffing it, scheduling a product, assessing the potential market, planning the sales campaign, and running a viable business for a set period of time. During the exercise decisions made by trainees are evaluated by 'umpires' (or computers): the results of one set of decisions influence the trainees' next set of decisions, and decisions made by one group affect the results of competing groups.

Business games require time (anything from 1-2 hours to several days) and the resources to run them effectively. They allow trainees to appreciate which key factors they must observe in order to understand the state of a business; they can learn about things like planning, budgeting, marketing, problem solving and decision taking. In addition, they can learn to appreciate the interdependence of various functions in an organisation and the importance of teamwork.

Good: business games give realistic experience of the techniques and skills needed to run an organisation, and trainees generally become very interested and involved.

Bad: 'playing games' may overshadow the learning experience, and too much reduction of the timespan in the situation can mean that the knowledge gained is only superficial.

The case-study method

For group training. A case study is a record of a real situation — including the surrounding facts, opinions and prejudices — given to trainees to analyse and discuss before deciding what action they would have taken. It may deal with a single event or with a situation involving a number of events. It may be presented in writing, orally, or in the form of film, filmstrips or slides. The method can be used to teach such subjects as administration, sales, industrial relations and human relations. It is especially useful in supervisory/management training for dealing with such concepts as authority and responsibility. Also, it can help trainees develop analytical ability and problem-solving and decision-taking skills.

Sometimes, along with the rest of the case history, details of the action which was taken are included. In such instances the trainees are asked to consider why that action was taken or to look at the alternative courses of action offered by the situation.

Good: trainees can draw upon experience and utilise skills which are a part of their work without incurring real risks.

Bad: unless the cases used are relevant to the needs and interests of the trainees they may be regarded as frivolous.

The incident method

For group training. This is a variation of the case-study method.

The case consists of a short statement of a real-life incident; for example, 'The chargehand found two operators fighting. One fell against a nearby machine and injured his arm. The chargehand reported the incident to the foreman.' Trainees have to seek further information by questioning the discussion leader before discussing the problem and deciding what action should be taken.

This method aims especially to inculcate in trainees the habit of asking questions and getting relevant information before determining the issues and taking a decision.

In this type of case discussion the leader supplies only the information requested, and should not interfere if trainees elect to decide on the basis of insufficient information: mistakes will become obvious when they have to justify their proposed actions. Organisation of the trainees into 'syndicates' adds a competitive element, which can increase involvement.

Good: as the incidents have actually happened, the action really taken can be compared with that proposed by the trainees; the trainees get practice in extracting and assessing information.

Bad: unless the discussion is carefully handled there is a risk the trainees may attach more importance to getting the 'right answer' — that is, 'winning the game' — than to learning the requisite skills.

Coaching

For individual training. Through coaching you can systematically increase the ability and experience of your staff by giving them carefully planned tasks in conjunction with continuous appraisal and counselling. Opportunities for coaching may arise because an individual requires improvement or because of changes in departmental or work procedures.

First you should agree a coaching plan and timetable with the trainee. You should select assignments or tasks that are relevant, and set high but attainable targets. Throughout, you should monitor progress, correcting if necessary and offering advice, guidance and encouragement. At the end of the coaching period you should review and evaluate the trainee's performance, and consider further development plans.

Good: coaching is a low-cost means of improving individual performance and departmental efficiency.

Bad: it is effective only if trainees can see its relevance and value to themselves as well as to their work, and if the coaching is carried out systematically and purposefully.

External courses

For individuals or groups. A wide variety of courses suitable for all types of employees are provided in technical, education subjects of which there is no knowledge or experience within the trainees' organisation, and opportunities for broadening individual experience. They are useful for meeting specific individual needs, when numbers are too small for an internal course (see below), or when employees cannot all be released at the same time.

If trainees are to benefit from one of these courses they must be briefed beforehand as to why they are attending and what they are expected to get out of it. After the course you should discuss with them the application of their new skills and knowledge so that further training and/or experience may enable trainees to put them into practice. This discussion can also be used to evaluate the course's effectiveness.

Good: external courses are ready-made, quick and easy to arrange, offer a wider choice of training facilities than can be provided internally, and give trainees the benefit of meeting people outside their own organisation who have different ideas and experience.

Bad: courses catering for a wide variety of trainees tend to be generalised, and the right course may not be available at the right time.

Internal courses

For group training. Courses for groups of employees in your department can be organised and conducted by yourself, by the organisation's training specialist, or with the help of an outside agency such as a technical or commercial college or a consultant. Whatever the means chosen, your involvement is essential for success. Not only are you able to pass on some of your knowledge and experience, the courses give you an opportunity to get to know what the trainees are doing and thinking about their own jobs. The feedback can provide some useful information concerning day-to-day practices and may also provide pointers for further training.

Good: such courses can be tailor-made for particular circumstances; a body of knowledge and skills is developed which is generally recognised and applied; trainees drawn from different units can get to know and understand one another and acquire a sense of identity; courses can be arranged when and where required.

Bad: unless you take care to include some sessions which inject new ideas there is a danger of 'inbreeding'.

Group discussion

In group training an interchange of ideas and experience guided to achieve the training objectives, can be used to help trainees learn from the knowledge and experience of others or to promote changes in opinions, attitudes, behaviour, and so on.

Control of the discussion depends mainly upon the guidance exercised by the discussion leader. To ensure that all trainees benefit from the time spent, leaders must prepare a plan. You should:

- analyse the subject and decide which aspects can or should be covered in the time available
- break down the subject matter into manageable steps
- prepare an introductory statement which defines the subject, explains the discussion plan, and includes an opening question to get the discussion off the ground.

Also, you need to keep the objectives clearly in mind and periodically focus the group's attention back onto them.

Good: this method gets trainees involved and committed; provides for cross-fertilisation of ideas and experience; gives trainees an opportunity to examine, test and perhaps change their own ideas, attitudes or behaviour.

Bad: unless well prepared and conducted, discussions can produce little more than muddled thinking and general frustration.

Job instruction

For individual training; adaptable for small groups. This involves a systematic four-step plan of instruction, and is mainly used for training in manual tasks, although it can be adapted for training in procedures and systems. The plan is:

- prepare the trainee: put them at their ease, spark their interest in learning the task, and check existing knowledge
- explain or demonstrate the task, one step at a time, stressing 'key points'; instruct clearly, completely, and at a pace the trainee can understand

- practise and test: get the trainee to do the task or explain the subject while you correct any errors and check understanding; continue until the required standard is achieved
- put the trainee to work but spot check from time to time.

Good: a simple, economical and efficient method of job training.
Bad: fine for simple tasks, but far less effective when the requirements are more complex.

Job rotation

For individual training. Trainees are moved into different jobs for short periods. They must be briefed as to what they are expected to learn, and their progress must be checked to make sure they actually benefit from the experience. The amount of responsibility they can be given at first depends on the extent and relevance of their previous experience. It is important that you select the jobs for their training potential and not just because they are short-term vacancies which it would be useful to fill.

Good: trainees acquire the specific practical experience they need quickly, instead of having to wait for opportunities to occur through promotions and transfers.
Bad: the right jobs may not be available at the right times; using or reserving specific jobs for training purposes can sometimes block other people's normal promotion chances.

Lectures

For group training. Lectures, with ensuing question-and-answer sessions, can be used to give new information, to introduce or summarise another piece of instruction, or to present a case for discussion.

Good: you can use a lecture to give information to a number of people at the same time.
Bad: misunderstandings can arise because you can't be sure the information is actually 'going in' (this problem can be overcome if you invite or ask questions during the lecture, so that you can adapt your material or approach accordingly).

Packaged programmes

Mainly for group training. Packaged programmes are available on a wide variety of subjects. They generally include a training manual, exercises and audiovisual aids, and assume the purchaser has or can hire the necessary equipment. The initial cost can be high, but may be worth it if the programme can be repeatedly used for groups.

Good: these can be very useful to managers, especially in organisations which have no training specialist, as all the hard work of collecting the material, planning the programme and getting together the instructional aids has been done.

Bad: you need to pick and choose, because attempts at adaptation can in some cases make the programmes less useful.

Programmed instruction

For individual training. The material appears in small, carefully sequenced segments ('frames'). Each frame elicits a response from the trainee, who is immediately told whether or not the response was correct. Two approaches are generally recognised:

- linear programming, in which one frame is so carefully constructed and validated that the learner will almost invariably give the correct response
- intrinsic or branching programming, which presents several possible responses from which learners select one; if they are correct they are given data for the next frame, but if they are wrong they are given further explanation and then given the chance to choose again.

Good: especially useful as a means of learning factual subjects.

Bad: less effective where training is concerned with promoting changes in opinions or behaviour or with the development of personal skills.

Role playing

For group training. Trainees are presented with a situation which they have to resolve by acting out the roles of the people involved. The method requires the setting up of a typical work scenario which trainees handle as they think appropriate. Their performance is observed and discussed by the trainer and the rest of the group. Role playing helps trainees recognise their own strengths and weaknesses, increase their appreciation of the differing attitudes and reactions of other people, improve their skill in dealing with people, and learn new techniques.

Role playing can be combined with other methods; for example, a case-study discussion concerning a disciplinary problem may be resolved by the trainees acting out the roles of boss and subordinates.

Good: trainees can practise skills and experiment in behaviour secure in the knowledge that they can make mistakes without having to face any of the consequences they would in real life.

Bad: the method can expose sensitive trainees to destructive criticism, or can disrupt personal relationships.

Special duties

For individual training. You can assign to trainees specific tasks which will enable them to acquire experience outside their normal job duties. Such activities might include representing the organisation on external bodies, membership of a professional or technical body, youth-club leadership, or attending trade meetings. These tasks should be carefully selected and assigned at various stages during the training programme.

Good: special duties can provide useful experience — especially for employees in line for supervisory or management jobs.

Bad: they may involve absence from normal job duties, and planning should take account of this.

Miscellaneous

Correspondence courses, guided reading and radio and TV programmes can all provide means of acquiring knowledge and skills applicable to a variety of jobs. Selection is important, and you must give the trainees some guidance as to how they should deal with the material. You should arrange for individual or group discussion to follow the reading, viewing, or whatever, and devise some tests (oral, written or practical) to assess what the trainees have learned.

Evaluation

Time and money spent on training are justified only if it contributes to the efficiency of the organisation and improves the performance and prospects of employees. Evaluation — to ensure the training has been worth it — is therefore mandatory. You should ask:

- did the results match up to the training objectives?
- what benefits did the organisation get?
- were there any useful spin-offs not directly related to the training objectives?
- what was the cost?
- how will decisions about future training be affected?

As well as making your own assessment you should ask the trainees how they felt they benefited from the training and get the views of other people who may have been involved — for example, other managers, supervisors or instructional staff.

Evaluation is comparatively simple for new entrants who had no previous experience of, say, operating a machine: if, after training, they can operate the machine safely and efficiently then the inference is obvious. But things get trickier when you're dealing with more complex jobs and with such skills as decision taking.

However, although in some cases you may have to rest your judgement on indicative evidence rather than proof, the evaluation of training is still worthwhile. Provided the objectives are identified in specific, measurable terms, you should be able to demonstrate 'cause and effect' quite clearly.

The training specialist

The function of the training specialist is to advise and assist line managers carry out their responsibilities for training and developing their subordinates. The specialist may be a full-time employee (in large organisations, training may require a whole department) or a senior executive who can undertake this function as part of his or her regular job. In either case, specialists can operate effectively only if they have your support and active involvement.

A competent training specialist can help you:

- analyse jobs
- prepare job descriptions
- prepare appraisal systems
- identify operational problems that training can solve

- plan the training programme
- give advice on selection of training methods, techniques and aids
- prepare training materials
- implement the training programme in specific areas delegated by management or in areas of particular complexity
- evaluate training
- prepare training budgets
- keep records
- train managers, supervisors and others in instructional techniques and skills
- keep managers informed of developments in the training field.

So it's worth keeping on the right side of your training specialist.

10 MANAGING CHANGE

Change is normal, but recently its rate has accelerated. For example, few people won't have been subject to some sort of structural change at work over the past few years and in many cases this will have happened several times. Technological advance over the past 20 years has been enormous, and its pace, too, has accelerated.

Our competitiveness depends upon our capacity to innovate and to keep pace with change. Our job, as individual managers and supervisors, is to manage change. That we do this well is vital for two reasons. First, we are employed to run effective organisations, and it is our job to do this well, whether or not we personally like the changes that are going on. Second, the satisfaction of those people for whom we are responsible depends upon our getting it right. So, for reasons of both efficiency and compassion, we must manage change properly.

How should we go about this? In this chapter we'll look at nine areas in which action is important. The actions themselves are commonsense, and familiar to us all, but all too often they are simply not carried out. Saying 'Sorry, I meant to consult you but there wasn't enough time' will not remedy the disruption caused by failing to consult. We must not only be conscious of the things we ought to do to manage change: we must actually do them.

Explaining change

Most difficulties in managing change seem to come about because of management's failure to communicate properly.

Employees work at their best when they are not just following orders but understand what is happening and why. If they understand the importance of their work — however humble or routine it may seem — they will not only give of their best, they will be willing to do so. This is the essence of motivation.

119

This is always true, but in times of rapid change the job of keeping people in the picture becomes more important — as well as more difficult. It becomes more important simply because there is more to tell the employees. And it becomes more difficult because many people instinctively fear any change — because they think it may adversely affect their working lives or those of their colleagues.

There are many examples of companies which have suffered considerable industrial problems purely because they failed to tell their employees what was going on. To take a specific example, a few years ago a London manufacturing company decided to subcontract some tooling — a move which did not, in fact, threaten anyone's job. However, the people in the tool-room first heard about the move 'through the grapevine' and, because management had failed to tell them about it, not unnaturally suspected the worst and came out on strike.

People in any organisation need to know what is going on. They need to know regularly, they need to be told face-to-face by their immediate boss, and they need to be informed relevantly. Regularity can be ensured by setting up a systematic drill so that, for example, everyone knows they will be briefed on the first Monday of each month at 9.30am. This briefing should be face-to-face with you, so that the staff can ask questions and so that you can make sure there are no misunderstandings. And the briefing should be relevant — that is, it should deal with subjects that will help raise the team's performance.

Any supervisor or manager can set up a system of this sort, but it makes more sense if briefing is coordinated throughout an organisation, or at least the whole of one site. This coordinated system of briefing — 'team briefing' — enables managers at more senior levels to get consistent and simultaneous messages to all employees.

Making this happen requires some extra action. A short management brief needs to be written, indicating clearly those items which are compulsory and those which are optional. This written brief should be given to everyone briefing staff, to make sure that the message does not become distorted. The timing of the briefings at each management level should be as close to simultaneous as possible, to avoid people picking up one version from their colleagues before they have heard what their own boss has to say.

Although the system should be company- or site-wide, the

primary aim is to put across information that is relevant to the particular group being briefed. At each level, at least 70 per cent of the briefing should be specific to the team.

Finally, the brief should be just that — brief. A briefing taking 20 minutes, plus 10 minutes for questions, should be plenty for most managers and supervisors. If more briefing is necessary, it is better to increase the frequency of briefing sessions (perhaps from once a month to once a week) than to increase their length. Almost everyone finds long meetings boring, and the purpose of these sessions is to get people on our side, not to turn them off.

Face-to-face communication is of paramount importance, but it also makes a lot of sense, especially during periods of change, to make sure that other systems are working well. For instance, is the notice-board up to date? And was there anything about the team structure in the company newsletter? So make someone responsible for keeping a weekly check on the notice-board and, if there is a newsletter, use it to communicate messages about local changes to the rest of the organisation.

Keeping control

Telling people what is going on is important — but it is vital, too, to know what is going on and to be able to influence it. If we are to exercise this influence our knowledge needs to be timely, relevant and accurate. In this area, haphazardness is a problem at the best of times, but during periods of change the problem can all too easily escalate until things are completely out of control. Worse still, we may not realise that this is happening until it is too late.

There are three main questions we must ask ourselves if we are to keep control during times of change.

First, is the ladder of accountability clear? Every person in the organisation should have a clear and singular answer to the question, 'Who is my boss?' If there is any uncertainty, it is not only confusing for the individual, it makes it much more difficult for us to keep any kind of check on what is going on. People should know exactly to whom they should report. Teams should not be too large — a manager or supervisor cannot adequately look after a team of more than about 15 people. Secretaries and personal assistants must be properly informed and not missed out because they are 'junior staff'. Administrative and support staff should know whether they should report to a senior administrator or to the technical/professional people they work for. Special attention must be paid to situations where people belong to a specific department but have been co-opted, pro tem, into a multidepartmental project team.

Clearly, most of us do not have the authority to revise the structures within which we work radically. However, if there seems to be some confusion we should discuss it, and try to sort out some more effective arrangement. For example, a supervisor put in control of 25 people might be able to ask the chargehand to look after 10 or 12 of them on a day-to-day basis.

The second question is: 'Do we see the individuals who work for us often enough to discuss their progress, consult them, and set targets?' Change may well mean that some people require more help and direction, because the demands of their jobs are changing. A regular 20 minutes with each team-member will help the whole team find solutions to their particular problems.

Third, what are the written records of progress like? We should have a single file that contains an up-to-date summary of the essential facts and figures, and it should always be ready to hand. And we should make certain that some individual is responsible for getting the weekly or monthly figures ready on time.

Ensuring commitment

Whatever measures you may take to keep control over events, the success or failure of change depends on the people who actually carry it out. As we have discussed, we should both keep people in touch and keep in touch with them, but what else can we do to ensure that, during change, what needs to be done is being done willingly and well?

The key is commitment.

It is important that people get a sense of achievement from their work, receive proper recognition when they do it well, know the importance of their work, and feel that their manager or supervisor listens to them. The problem is that, in reality, work is often boring and mundane, and that supervisors and managers have only limited time — especially during periods of change.

Delegation (*see* Chapter 5) is an immensely valuable tool which can both save your time and help motivate your staff. But do not use it just as a way of ridding yourself of a series of tedious chores. It is much better to delegate a sizeable chunk of authority to an individual than to give that person a series of one-off tasks. Few people enjoy trivial chores, but most people get satisfaction from doing a large and difficult job well, even if that job involves those same trivial chores.

Target setting (*see* Chapter 4) is useful, because it provides a challenge: people get satisfaction from achieving against the odds (although the targets should not be impossible). For similar reasons, clarify what is to be done and, if possible, show people the end-product of their labours, whether it be a physical object or a service.

If at all possible, consult everyone who might be affected by one of your decisions (*see* Chapter 6). An ideal time to do this is at your regular team briefings. Consultation does not necessarily mean you have to compromise: it just shows that you are prepared to listen to other people's views and then either accept or reject them. Often, of course, you will find that their views help you make a better decision, but, even if this is not the case, your staff will have had the satisfaction of saying what they think.

A final point on motivation. Try to ensure that, as circumstances change, people's pay and working conditions do not suffer, and that everyone receives equitable treatment. During change, it is even more important than usual that grievances receive prompt attention.

Coaching individual performance

It is our job to coach and advise our people through change.

As we know, it is important to see subordinates regularly on a one-to-one basis. Such meetings can be used to assess and review individual performance. Annual performance reviews and appraisal systems are important, as we saw in Chapter 3, but more frequent review is often a good thing — and virtually essential in times of change, when jobs and job objectives are changing rapidly. At such times, there may be some confusion as to who is an individual's boss: if structures have changed or if people have been doing work for other managers, consult those other managers first but, when it comes down to it, stick to a one-to-one discussion.

There are five other main questions which, though usually unvoiced, need to be answered.

What is my job?

It is vital that both you and the job-holder have a compatible view of what results should be expected. Of course, jobs are dynamic, and it would be silly to wait for formal discussion before doing what has to be done; however, we need to keep ourselves informed and make sure the right things are being done in the right way.

What standard is expected?

Give people yardsticks by which they can assess their own performance. These yardsticks cannot always be quantified — the volume of work done may be less important than its quality — but they should be put forward and regularly updated so that priorities do not become confused.

How am I getting on?

Often people don't know. Simply by clarifying standards you will help people get a better idea of their own performance. At the same time, you can learn from good work (and praise it) and identify areas of difficulty, from discussion of which you and the job-holder may be able to work out a better way of doing things.

Where do I go in the future?

An honest discussion of expected changes before they happen can help to avoid sudden gaps appearing between available skills and required tasks (although, of course, you should not fall into the trap of raising expectations and then failing to fulfil them). If you do not coach and develop existing staff you may find that you unexpectedly have to 'buy in' outside skills — which is an expensive, and potentially disruptive, practice.

How do I get there?

Once current and future positions have been discussed, targets need to be set — set, not agreed, because it is your job to make the final decision. However, the most sensible targets are usually those based on the job-holder's own ideas, so consult him or her first. Do not set too many targets: setting five or six will help clarify priorities, but setting 23 will not. Avoid setting all the deadlines for the same date.

Taking decisions and delegating

In times of change, on-the-spot decisions are often required. These may seem small in themselves, but their effects, because they have deadlines attached, may be deleterious to other important work. Likewise, during times of change delegation can be difficult — because, in the short term, it is often easier to do the work yourself than to explain it to someone else. What is needed is a systematic approach to both problems.

First, delegate early. Before change accelerates, subordinates should have the preparation necessary to cope with it. Constructive use of performance coaching (*see* page 107) will help. Try to avoid interfering with people to whom you have delegated work: remember that decisions taken 'on the job' are usually better than those taken from an ivory tower. Set up a sensible monitoring system, have an occasional impromptu look at what is going on, and take the risk.

If there is something that you cannot delegate, how should you approach a decision? First, consider how soon the decision needs to be taken: the longer you have, the more relevant facts you can assemble to help you decide. Also, consult anybody who may be affected by your decision — and even people who will not be affected but who might have some helpful ideas.

Once you have done these things, decide. Sleep on it if there is time. Then, once you have made your decision, tell everybody about it. Tell as many people as possible face-to-face and, if they need to pass the news down the line, issue a written version, too.

Finally, check that your decision has been carried out. Staff will soon realise if you are the sort of boss who issues instructions but fails to follow them up.

In an emergency, of course, you may have to short-circuit the process, which may mean that you should be delegating more. Whatever the case, make sure everyone is informed of your decision as soon as possible.

Training for change

Training (*see* Chapter 9) is a matter of survival. If organisations are to adapt, so must the people working within them. This must be explained to everyone, and they must be shown how to go about this process of adaptation.

It is all too easy to see training as a specialist function, divorced from the normal duties and responsibilities of managers and supervisors. There are, however, three compelling reasons for thinking hard about training. First, most of what we learn we learn by doing: structured experience provides the most effective means of raising levels of skill and knowledge. Second, the level of ability of our team is of direct consequence to us, and therefore we should be keen to raise it as much as possible. Third, change demands a quick training response: local initiative is required if this response is to be fast enough.

Information is, as always, important. It is often a good idea to keep a file of who can do what, including details of individuals' formal internal and external training courses as well as information about their 'on the job' training.

Do not try to do all the local training yourself: you are unlikely to have the time to do it properly, and anyway there may be people in your team — or elsewhere in your organisation — who could do it better.

Formal training courses, if available, are often useful (*see* page 112). However, much of the benefit will be lost if the training is not applied properly to the work itself. In order to counter this danger, find out exactly what the course teaches and how, brief trainees on what you expect them to get out of the course, and debrief them when they return: the trainees may know better than you how to put the training to best effect, and may also now have the abilities to pass on the training to others.

You may, of course, find some resistance to training. This might be simply fear of the unknown, but it could represent a genuine difficulty in adapting to the demands of a changed job. Frequent coaching sessions may help solve the former problem: people who find the prospect of radical change daunting may find it easier to accept it in the form of a series of smaller-scale changes. This is often particularly so with experienced people, who are being asked to change long-established methods and patterns of work. The problem of inability to adapt is more difficult. Every effort should be made in training and counselling to help such people either adapt or find new roles within the organisation, but you have to accept that, during a time of change, some redundancy may be unavoidable.

What about the unions?

Trade unions are often depicted as being resistant to change, and occasionally they are, but vast areas of industry, commerce and the public services have gone through major structural or technological change without significant industrial-relations problems. We in management must identify what we can do to develop and maintain constructive relations with the unions during periods of change. Having the union on our side may not just 'allow' us to effect change: the union may positively help us.

When we look at past instances where it has proved difficult to get union cooperation during times of change, one issue crops up again and again: communication. To take a classic example, a large local authority wanted to introduce job evaluation at the same time as reductions in overall staffing. Despite regular consultative meetings, this innovation was not mentioned to the employees until it had started. As a result, the employees refused to cooperate not only on this issue but on others, and the scheme's introduction was delayed by several months.

Two lines of communication need working on. First, we need to establish good, regular communication through the management line, as discussed above. We cannot expect the unions to deliver our message for us — it is not their job. Second, we need a systematic way of consulting staff and their representatives and, where appropriate, of negotiating with them.

Of crucial importance is the relationship between front-line supervision and union representatives. If these two see each other regularly and are used to sorting out problems themselves, minor grievances (an almost inevitable product of change) can be sorted out before they develop into major issues. To this end, it may be useful to provide some training for both supervisors and representatives.

Where consultative committees exist, managers should use them — not just to assess reactions to imminent change but also to garner ideas about how to go about things in a way that favours everyone's best interests. Make sure that any management plans announced at these meetings are already being explained to managers and supervisors; otherwise managers will discover their boss's proposals from their subordinates.

If you want to change terms and conditions of work, start early. Negotiating against a tight deadline may mean you have to give way on some issues where actually you should stand firm.

All of this assumes the existence of clear written procedural agreements. Have a look at these, and check that they are robust and sensible enough to work when change is going on at pace.

Staying in touch

At the bottom of organisations, change is often seen as something done by 'them' to 'us'. One way of making sure this attitude does not prevail is for us to find out what life is like at the bottom of our organisation.

The larger the organisation and the more senior the manager, the greater the risk of losing touch with the shop-floor (or equivalent). In periods of rapid change this problem gets worse. It may seem to us that there is simply too much to do to have time to maintain human contact with the people for whom we are responsible. However, we need both to see and to be seen; we must make the time.

As we saw in Chapter 1, you should regularly walk the job. You should visit not just the people who report to you but also the people who report to your subordinate managers and supervisors. This is not intended to undermine the intermediate leaders, but to help you know better what is going on. Indeed, it is bad practice to interfere, except in an emergency such as a physically dangerous working habit.

When things are changing quickly, increase the frequency of your walkabouts. If the offices were rearranged at the weekend, check to see how they look on the Monday morning. Ask people how they feel about the new arrangements. Walk the job on the night shift. Check how well people are kept informed by their immediate bosses; for example, how positively have the changes been explained to them?

Another thing you should be doing is working alongside people. If you are the immediate team leader, you should count this as a regular and frequent part of your job. If new tasks have to be undertaken, find out for yourself how difficult, boring or time-consuming they are. Show that you care about the physical conditions people work in. Even if you're a more senior manager you should still do this from time to time: apart from the fact that you'll be making a good impression, you will find out things when working alongside someone which you would never be told in any other situation.

Do not just plan to do this: do it. Good intentions are not enough. If you simply try to 'fit it in', it will never happen. Decide on the frequency of such excursions, and block off time in your diary. When changes are in progress, make sure that you are seen around both during and immediately after the more radical ones.

During times of change, attend (and if necessary arrange) social functions with your staff. You may not want to, but it is a part of your job — as is looking as if you're enjoying yourself. Even if the change is one forced by economic difficulties, try to organise some sort of social event — although, if things are tight, this should be self-financing: people quite naturally resent subsidised parties at a time when some of them are being made redundant for lack of funds.

Learning from change

Change inevitably involves risk and experiment. However good our planning, success cannot be guaranteed. So we should be prepared to alter our plans. We are not doing our jobs properly if we are simply monitoring the effects of change: anyone can monitor failure. We lose credibility in the eyes of our staff if we remain wedded to an unworkable idea simply because we thought of it.

It is helpful to determine a review period. If we are changing structures in some parts of the organisation, we should set up a meeting of the accountable managers for, say, three months after the changes. Ask yourself, and the managers, some pertinent questions. Are we achieving what we intended to achieve? Are results better? Could the changes be still further improved? Should similar changes be made elsewhere in the organisation?

There are, of course, occasions when the answers will indicate that the best thing to do is to scrap the changes, and we should do something different or revert to the old system immediately, before we waste any more time and money. Do not be afraid to face this fact.

Avoid inventing the wheel twice. Inevitably there will be teething troubles, but, if a change in one part of an organisation eventually works out well, get the details written down so that people in other parts of the organisation can learn from both your successes and your mistakes.

Make sure changes of plan are explained as soon as possible to everyone likely to be affected. True, it may be difficult, if you have enthused about one scheme, to be equally convincing about a radical alteration to it — but you have to do so if you are to have any chance of seeing the changes carried out well. Always, you should explain why the plan is being changed: people may well resent policy-shifts unless they know the reasons for them. If you do not know the reasons yourself, pester your boss until you do.

APPENDIX: CHECKLISTS

Checklist: motivating

- Have you agreed with each of your subordinates his or her main targets and continuing responsibilities, together with standards of performance, so that you can both recognise achievement?
- Do you recognise the contribution of each member of the group and encourage other team members to do the same?
- In the event of success, do you acknowledge it and build on it? In the event of setbacks, do you identify what went well and give constructive guidance for improving future performance?
- Can you delegate more? Can you give more discretion over decisions and more accountability to a subgroup or individual?
- Do you show to those who work with you that you trust them, or do you hedge them around with unnecessary controls?
- Are there adequate opportunities and (where necessary) retraining?
- Do you encourage each individual to develop his or her capacities to the full?
- Is the overall performance of each individual regularly reviewed in face-to-face discussion?
- Does financial reward match contribution?
- Do you make sufficient time to talk and listen, so that you understand the unique (and changing) profile of needs and wants in each person, so that you can work with the grain of nature rather than against it?
- Do you encourage able people with the prospect of promotion within the organisation, or — if that is impossible — counsel them to look elsewhere for the next position fitting their merit?
- Can you think of a manager by name who delegates (a) more effectively or (b) less effectively than you do? What are the results in the case of both (a) and (b)?

Checklist: organising

Organising is an important function in meeting the requirements of all three circles in the leadership model.

Group
- Is the size of the working group correct, and are the right people working together?
- Is there a need for subgroups to be constituted?
- Are there regular opportunities or procedures for genuine consultation with the group before taking decisions affecting them — for example, decisions relating to work plans and output, work methods and standards, work measurement and overtime working?

Organisation
- Are you clear on the purpose of the organisation and how the various parts of it work together to achieve that end?
- Is there an effective system for staffing the organisation and training? Is there a fair dismissal procedure?
- Do you carry out regular surveys of the organisation to check (a) size of all working groups, (b) number of leadership levels, (c) growth of unnecessary complexity, (d) line and staff cooperation, and (e) that communication systems are working properly?

Yourself
- Are there ways in which you could organise your personal and working life—for example, where you live—in order to be a more effective leader?
- Do you delegate sufficiently?
- Have you identified at least three steps you can take in order to become a better organiser of your time?

Checklist: setting an example

- Which of these statements would you say most applies to you?
    - (a) People often comment on the good example you set in your work. You never ask others to do what you are not willing to do yourself.
    - (b) Sometimes your bad example conflicts with all that we are trying to do here.
    - (c) You are not really aware of the importance of example and are unable to say what kind of one you are giving.
- On what occasion(s) in the last months have you deliberately set out to give a lead by your example?
- Did your action have any effect on the group or individual, either (a) immediately or (b) some days later?
- What specific problems in the area of team maintenance might you help to solve by giving a better personal example yourself?
- If you are a senior leader or appraiser of other leaders, have you mentioned to others the importance of example in leadership during the last three months?
- Using the 'brainstorming' approach (see page 74), can you produce three new—more creative — ways in which you and more senior leaders in the organisation might set an example?

Checklist: does your organisation develop leaders?

- Do you have a clear strategy for building good human relations which includes developing leadership at every level?
- When selecting people for management jobs, do you assess them in terms of their functional ability (task, team and individual) and the associated qualities of personality and character?
- Are appointed leaders given a minimum of two days of leadership training?
- Do you have some system for career development, so that future senior leaders broaden their experience and knowledge?
- Are all line managers convinced that they are the real leadership trainers, however effective they are in that role?
- Is there a specialist 'research and development' team who are keeping the organisation and its line managers up to date—and up to the mark?
- Has your organisational structure been evolved with good leadership in mind?
- Do leaders, actual or potential, realise that they are the ones who 'own' the problem of self-development?
- Would you say that there was room for improving the organisational ethos? None at all, some, or a very great deal?
- Is your top person and his or her key team really behind leadership development?

Checklist: your leadership self-development programme

- Have you drafted a programme of action or growth points which covers the
    short term (up to 12 months)?
    medium term (1-3 years)?
    long term (4-10 years)?
- Have you entered in your diary some dates for progress reviews?
- Can you discuss your plans with anyone at work or outside it to establish if they are, perhaps, too ambitious, too modest, too vague or too unrealistic?
- What would you say is the key sentence in this book as far as you are concerned? Write it down on a sheet of paper.
- Are you prepared to read that sentence again in six months' time to see if it has had any effect on your leadership?

Checklist: briefing

- Do you regularly brief your group on the organisation's current plans and future developments?
- Would you rate yourself as good, adequate or weak on each of these five skills of effective briefing?
    preparing?
    clarifying?
    simplifying?
    vivifying?
    being yourself?
- Can you think of a few specific ways in which you could improve your skills?
- Could your organisation improve its two-way communication of information and instructions with those responsible for carrying them out?

Checklist: are you right for the situation?

- Do you feel that your interests, aptitudes (for example, mechanical and verbal) and temperament are suited to the field you are in?
- Can you identify a field in which you would be more likely to emerge as a leader?
- How have you developed the 'authority of knowledge'? Have you done all you can at this stage in your career to acquire the necessary professional or specialist training available?
- Have you experience in more than one field or more than one industry or more than one function?
- Do you take an interest in fields adjacent to your own and potentially relevant?
- How flexible are you within your field? Is your flexibility, in terms of the list below, (a) good, (b) adequate or (c) weak?
    - (a) Do you respond to situational changes with marked flexibility of approach, read situations well, think about them and respond with the appropriate kind of leadership?
    - (b) Although you may have proved yourself in a couple of situations, do you in fact fear other situations? Are you happiest only when the situation is normal and predictable?
    - (c) Are you highly adapted to one particular work environment and unable to stand change? Are you often described by your colleagues as rigid and inflexible?

Checklist: do you have some basic leadership qualities?

- List the five key characteristics or personal qualities which are expected or required in workers in your field. How do you rate yourself in each of them — good, average or weak?
- Where would you place yourself on a continuum running from 'very introvert' to 'very extrovert'? (Leaders tend to be 'ambiverts' — a mixture of both introvert and extrovert, but with rather more extrovert than introvert qualities.)
- Have you shown yourself to be a responsible person?
- Do you like the responsibility as well as the rewards of leadership?
- Are you self-sufficient enough to withstand criticism, indifference or unpopularity from others and to work effectively with others without constant supervision?
- Are you an active and socially participative person?
- Can you control your emotions and moods — or do they control you?
- Have you any evidence to suppose that other people see you as essentially a warm person?
- Can you give instances from the past three months where you have been deliberately dishonest or less than straight with the people who work with you?
- Are you noted for your enthusiasm at work?
- Has anyone ever used the word 'integrity' in relation to you?

Checklist: the three circles

- Have you been able to give specific examples from your own experience on how the three circles or areas of need — task, group and individual—interact with each other?
- Can you identify your natural bias:
    - (a) Do you tend to put the task first, being poor on group and individual concerns?
    - (b) Do you think the group is most important, so that you value happy relations more than productivity or individual job satisfaction?
    - (c) Do you tend to put the individual before the task of the group, and over-identify with the individual?
    - (d) Can you honestly say you maintain a balance, and have feedback from colleagues, superiors and subordinates to prove it?
- Do you vary your social distance from the group according to a realistic appreciation of the factors in the situation?
- Can you illustrate from experience your answer to the previous question?

Checklist: planning your work

- Have you called upon specialist advice before making your plan?
- Did you consider all the feasible courses of action and weigh them up in terms of resources needed/available and outcomes?
- Have you a programme now which will achieve your objective?
- Is there a provision for contingencies?
- Did you and the group actively search for a more creative solution as the basis for your plan?
- Have you made the plan as simple and as foolproof as possible, rather than complicated?
- Does the plan include any necessary preparation or training of the group or individuals?

Checklist: defining the task

- Are you clear about the objectives of your group now and for the next few years/months, and have you agreed them with your boss?
- Do you fully understand the wider aims and purpose of the organisation?
- Can you relate the objectives of your group to those larger, more general intentions?
- Does your present main objective have sufficient specificity? Is it defined in terms of time? Is it as concrete or tangible as you can make it?
- Will the group soon be able to know for themselves if you succeed or fail? Does it have swift feedback of results?

Checklist: controlling

- Do you maintain a balance between controlling with too tight a rein and giving the group too much freedom to do as it pleases?
- Are you able to coordinate work in progress, bringing all the several parts into a common, harmonious action in proper relation with each other?
- On those occasions when you are directly involved with the 'technical' work, do you make arrangements so that the team requirements and the specific needs of its members are not ignored or overlooked?
- Can you list the three characteristics of the most effective chairman of meetings you have come across?
- When you are 'in the chair', do meetings never, sometimes or always run over the time allotted for them?
- Does your department or unit have a proper budgeting system?
- Is the organisation you work for noted with customers on account of its control systems in the following areas?
  quality of product/service?
  delivery?
  keeping costs down?
  safety?

Checklist: evaluating

- In assessing the outcome of possible courses of action or solutions do you take time to consider the consequences for the team and the individual as well as the task?
- How do you rate yourself as far as judgement in decision making is concerned — (a) good, (b) average, or (c) weak?
    - (a) Your decisions usually have the predicted results. You can foresee consequences and are rarely surprised at outcomes. You are shrewd and discerning at all times.
    - (b) Your predictions of consequences are accurate about half the time. Your common sense is often proved right.
    - (c) Poor judgement often mars your performance. You tend to guess too much what will result from a given decision, and are frequently wrong.
- How would you assess yourself as an appraiser of the work of an individual? Are you (a) good at it, (b) average at it, or (c) weak at it?
    - (a) you hold regular appraisal meetings and do quite a lot on a day-to-day basis. You always support general points with evidence. You tend always to praise first and criticise second. Your appraising usually results in better work performance.
    - (b) Sometimes it seems to work, other times not. You find it difficult to hit the right note with some people. Quite frankly, awkward people, who do not want to learn, defeat you.
    - (c) You lose credibility every time you try to appraise someone. It usually ends up in an argument. You tell them, but they refuse to listen.
- What is your record in judging people? In selecting and promoting individuals, which of the following statements best characterises your approach?
    - (a) You can always pick a winner, and never consult anyone else or seek specialist advice.

(b) You go by first impressions. Even if you think you are wrong, you usually return to them in the end.

(c) You take 'people decisions' slowly. You like to consult, often on a confidental basis, others who know the person. You do not trust your own first thoughts.

(d) You like to see a person in a variety of different situations before making up your mind. Track record is an important factor to you — more so than psychological tests and the like.

(e) You rarely choose a person on technical grounds alone, unless they are working on their own. You try to see them in the context of their being a team leader or member, and to judge if they will get on well with the individuals in that group.

- Would you regard your regular evaluation of your own performance as (a) more rigorous, (b) less searching, or (c) about the same as your evaluation of others?

INDEX

appraisal interviews 26, 36
changed by delegation 52, 56
recruitment 88, 89, 90, 92-3, 97
secretaries 83
skills 86
Job instruction 113-4
Job rotation 114
Job satisfaction
as an incentive 2, 4
effect of change 119, 123
effect of training 102

Leaders
experience 7
influence of 2, 121
Leadership 1-3, 131-2
Learning
by doing 126
from change 129
leadership 131

McGregor, Douglas 13-4
Management
by consent 69
by exception 60-1
by objectives 28-9, 34, 37
levels 21-3, 45
structures 32
Managers
line 23, 29, 87, 127
middle 22, 80, 128
senior 21-2
top 21-2
training 70
Maslow, Abraham 13, 14
Measurement
performance 38-9, 45-6
work 19
Meetings
consultative 127
failures 81
time taken 79-80
Membership of unions 98
Merit awards 26

Merit rating 28
Mistakes
acknowledgment 71
delegated tasks 58-60, 64, 80
selection (recruitment) 101
Monitoring
change 20, 122, 125
decisions 68-9
performance 45
training 102, 116-7, 126
Morale
achieving objectives 3
effects of delegation 50
Motivation
change 19-21, 119-21, 123
decision taking 64, 70
effect of delegation 48, 50
failures 93
individual workers 4, 11-2
praise 59
self 13

National Institute of Industrial Psychology 89
Needs of individual workers 13, 25
New staff
checklists 104-5
experience 103
first day 101
performance 106
physical requirements 90
private circumstances 91-2
qualifications 91
teams 87
training 101, 103, 106, 117

Objectives
achieving 3
appraisal 35
briefing 30
clarification 30, 41
commitment 24
communication 30

148